Copyright © 2018 by Goldia Felder

All rights reserved. No part of this publication may be reproduced, distributed, or transmitted in any form or by any means, including photocopying, recording, or other electronic or mechanical methods, without the prior written permission of the publisher, except in the case of brief quotations embodied in critical reviews and certain other noncommercial uses permitted by copyright law.

Printed in the United States of America

Edited by SMP Editing Services
smpeditingservices@gmail.com

PAINTED LIES

Goldia Felder

Dedicated to...

This book is dedicated to all the women of the "Me, Too" movement. Sexual abuse, harassment and rape is never okay. Silence and denial is never the answer. It takes courage to come forward and use your voice in protest against sexual abuse in all its forms. Whether on a college campus, in the work place, our homes or elsewhere, we have the right to not only feel safe, but to be safe. We have the right to say no and without exception have that "no" be respected and honored.

Contents

Prologue
7

1 The Unveiling of Innocence
12

2 The Coldness Creeps In
26

3 The Search for Tranquility
52

4 Forsaking The Memories
77

5 The Brittle Steps We Take
103

6 Crumbling Beneath Her Feet
125

7 A Volatile Turn
147

8 A Shattered Rose
177

9 Delusions May Come
200

Epilogue
224

PAINTED

LIES

~ Prologue ~

Marisa, a senior at Tillis University, drummed her fingers on the counter top of the Office of Academics. Her best friend, a feisty young African-American girl, sat nervously on the steps of the student building.

Suddenly, Marisa ran from the student academic's office and out the double doors of the building, laughing. Waving a letter in her hand, she called out to her friend, Tiffany, who upon hearing her voice, turned to see her running down the stairs to where she sat.

"Tiffany! Tiffany! I got it! I got the internship at Brusselton's!"

Tiffany stood up smiling and clapping her hands.

"I can't believe it!" Marisa grabbed her, hugging her neck in excitement.

"I'm so proud of you!" Tiffany said as they jumped up and down in celebration.

"Oh my gosh, Marisa…London! You got an internship in freaking London!"

"I know!" she said, a bit winded. Suddenly, she yelled out how much she loved her life as she twirled around at the bottom of the steps. "Now, to just get through tonight," she said looking down at her watch. A look of distress suddenly crossed her face.

"What?! What's wrong?"

Marisa tapped her watch with her finger. *That couldn't be the time*, she thought, as she brought her cell phone up to confirm the time.

Tiffany's eyes widened. They looked across the campus lawn before taking off towards the school's auditorium. In anticipation of Marisa's news, they had forgotten about the practice run for their commencement exercise.

Running as fast as their feet could carry them, they dodged one obstacle after another. Tiffany and Marisa ran around students like seasoned football players. With head down and taking two steps a time, Marisa bumped into one of the campus students. It was Patrick, the Valedictorian of their senior class.

"Whoa!" Patrick said as he held Marisa at her shoulders. "Late again I see."

Patrick was referring to a foreign language class that he and Marisa had taken together. She never seemed to be able to get to that class on time.

"No, we're just trying to make sure we get to the auditorium on time."

Patrick looked at his watch. "Well, I don't think you're going to make it."

"And what makes you say that?" Tiffany said, butting into the conversation. "If my memory serves me correctly, Mr. Weston, you're supposed to be there, too. Or did you just find out that you flunked? Awwww."

Tiffany and Marisa chuckled as they made their way up the stairs and into the auditorium.

The band members were packing up their instruments while the faculty was finishing up last minute details on the stage. Just as Marisa and Tiffany threw open one of the doors, they noticed students walking out. They looked at each other, then continued slowly down the stairs.

"Oh my gosh, Tiff, we missed rehearsal!"

A voice came from behind them. "Yep, looks like you did."

They turned to see Patrick seated in one of the auditorium chairs. On the step above him stood Matthew Collins, one of the wide receivers of the football team.

"Hey there, lil ladies," he said as he clinched a camel colored cowboy's hat between his fingers and nodded.

Marisa walked back up the steps to where Patrick sat.

"Why didn't you tell me the rehearsal was over?" Swatting him on the shoulder.

"I just wanted the satisfaction of seeing your faces when you realized you'd missed it. Priceless," Patrick chuckled.

Marisa looked up at Matthew who was also laughing. "I don't think it's funny, you jerks."

By this time Tiffany had come up and grabbed Marisa by the arm. "Come on *Miss Uncongeniality*. Let's go get something to eat. I'm hungry," she tugged Marisa along as they headed out of the auditorium. "Let's take my car. I'm scared of your driving," Tiffany said as she unlocked the car door. "Why do you always get so defensive? You know Patrick is a jokester."

"He just rubs me the wrong way, that's all." She locked her seatbelt.

"Girl, you need to loosen up. How long has it been?"

She looked over at Tiffany. "How long since what?"

"You know, since…" she gestured.

"Tiffany!" Marisa punched her in the shoulder.

"What?! Why did you punch me?"

"Oh, don't play innocent. I know what you meant."

Tiffany took a quick glance at her. "Girl, you need to get your mind out the gutter.

"Ooo! Let's go to the food court at the mall," Marisa suggested.

They sat in the food court talking and reminiscing about their time at Tillis. Oddly, the bad times and the inconsistencies didn't seem all that important anymore. For a moment they sad quietly, almost somber. Graduation had become a reality. Soon their time at Tillis University would become a memory for them both. Oddly enough, even the lows and inconsistencies of college life they had experienced would be missed.

Drinking her soft drink, Tiffany burst into laughter.

Even though Marisa had no clue why, she couldn't help but laugh at her friend's outburst. "What?! What's so funny."

Tiffany tried to regain her composure. "Remember when we were pledging and they told us to beat down the

Commons Area wall? You looked at me like...how are we going to do that? The look on your face was priceless. You didn't realize all we had to do was start from the top and go to the bottom."

"Oh, yeah, I remember that. Here I was thinking they meant literally. I remember thinking these sorority girls are crazy!"

Tiffany laughed herself to tears. "Come on, Rissa, let's go. One thing I'm not going to be late for is my graduation. Traffic is going to be hell today with all that's going on."

Tiffany cranked the car and began backing out. She heard the horn of an approaching car and quickly hit her brakes, stopping the car with a jerk. "See, I told you, girl. I can't even get out of the parking lot." She started laughing again. "I remember the time this man cut your mom off right before the traffic light. The light turned red and your mom pulled right up beside him, rolled her window down and asked him if he was in a hurry."

"Oh yes, I remember that really well. I slid down in the seat I was so embarrassed."

Tiffany gasped as she looked over at Marisa. "What?! Embarrassed?! Honey I was like get him Mrs. Webb. Girl, I didn't know she could be so feisty."

"Yeah, if only she was," Marisa said somberly.

Tiffany noticed her mood change. "Um, was it something I said?"

Marisa shook her head. "Tiffany, you know, Mom is an amazing woman. Sometimes I wonder why she is so docile."

"Docile?! Who Mrs. Webb?! We must be talking about two different people."

"I wish we were. Mom just seems to be willingly blind to...well, to things."

"Things like what? Come on, girl, I'm your best friend. You can talk to me," Tiffany said as she parked the car in the parking lot of their dorm.

With misty eyes, Marisa looked over at Tiffany.

"Hey, like whoa! It can't be that serious, Rissa. Don't cry."

She affectionately rubbed on her friend's shoulder in an effort to console her. Gathering her composure, Marisa softly sniffled as she took a deep breath.

"No, I'm not. Nothing is going to dampen this day. I'm graduating college and headed to London," she said with a low energy of excitement in her voice.

Tiffany cleared her throat.

"Excuse me, correction. We're graduating college. As in me and you," motioning back and forth with two fingers. Her antics made Marisa laugh.

"Okay, *we* are graduating." Marisa looked down at her watch again. "But if we don't get out of this car, we both won't be tonight."

They laughed as they got out of the car and headed to get ready for a graduation night they would never forget.

1

The Unveiling of Innocence

It was early fall. A few blocks away from Marisa's dorm sat the college that she had attended for the past four years. The campus was bustling with the seniors of Tillis University, gathering with their family and friends for their long awaited walk across their alma mater's stage. They had studied and worked very hard to achieve their dreams, and this was the moment the students had long awaited for. Their time had come and a new future was about to begin.

The street that ran in front of Marisa's dorm hadn't been this busy since the university's homecoming and stomp competition between sororities and fraternities of the college alumni. Everywhere you looked students ran from all directions. Some were holding their caps close to their heads as they sprinted by, their gowns waving in the wind like a freed wild stallion behind them. The sound of horns filled the air as campus volunteers directed drivers to designated parking spaces.

You could hear the sound of band members as they warmed up their instruments for the night's commencement exercise. Members of the chorus group sang melodies and ran up and down the vocal scale to loosen up their voices.

Marisa had made it back to her dorm. The elevator door was in constant motion with the massive influx of people that were on campus. Chattering voices filled the dormitory.

"Marisa! Hurry up, honey, we'll be late!"

Her mother paced back and forth along the cluttered co-ed dorm that Marisa had lived in for the past two years with two other roommates.

"Where's Dad, Mom!" she asked from the entrance of the bathroom door where she nervously put on her makeup. "Is he coming?!"

Marisa hopped through the bathroom door with one shoe in hand while trying to put on the other.

"I don't know. He was still at the office when I spoke to him last."

Marisa stopped dressing immediately. Disappointed, she looked at her mother. "What?! At the office?! This is my college graduation day, Mom!"

"I know dear," her mother said, looking at her. The tone of her voice was full of empathy. "You know how your father is. He's been working a lot, dear. Now, come on, Marisa," her mother said as she grabbed her blue purse that had been lying on the green floral couch.

Angrily, Marisa grabbed her graduation gown. She had set it on the arm of the sofa some time earlier. "I will hate him if he doesn't make it to my graduation," she said as she stood in the doorway.

"He'll be there, dear. I'm sure," her mother said as she eased around Marisa and walked out the door.

Marisa closed the door behind her, and locked it. They headed down the corridor to the elevator. Once they were inside she hit the button for the first floor.

"Hey! Hey! Hold the elevator!"

It was Patrick Weston.

He was a six-foot three college athlete and captain of the college's football team for the last two seasons. He and Marisa had taken foreign language studies by the same professor. He would be graduating cum laude with an engineering degree. They had lived in the same dorm for the past year. Well-known around campus, Marisa saw him mostly as arrogant and cocky—the typical attitude of most athletes, she thought.

Patrick jumped onto the elevator just before the doors closed.

"Trying to get yourself flattened before you graduate?" Marisa was still annoyed from the news that her father may not make it to the graduation.

"Nope. I want to graduate in one piece. Don't you?" Patrick said as he honed in on Marisa's tone and body language. "But it does sound like you're trying to get the *best mean girl* award."

"What does that mean?" she turned towards him.

He leaned back against the elevator doors. His graduation gown was draped across his left shoulder. His cap was slightly slanted to one side of his head. With his arms folded, he looked at Marisa and gave her a slight smirk. Her mother stood quietly as the young man and her daughter continued bating each other.

"Fille moyenne," *Mean girl,* Patrick said to her in French.

Marisa was ready respond when the doors of the elevator opened all of a sudden, catching Patrick off guard. He lost his balance and hit the floor with a hard thud. She laughed.

"Oh, cette secousse mal fait?" *Oh, did that hurt, jerk?* she replied in French.

Patrick struggled to get up. Picking his cap and gown up from the floor, he clumsily struggled to get his footing as he slipped again hitting the floor.

"Oh my! Are you alright, son?" her mother looked at him with a look of concern.

Marisa stepped over him. Her mother maneuvered her way around Patrick's feet that were still partly inside the elevator.

"Come on, Mom, I don't want to be late. Mr. Weston will be fine. Nothing's hurt but his ego." She smirked at him as she and her mother headed towards the exit door of the building.

Concerned, Marisa's mother looked back to see if he had gotten up off the floor. "Are you sure you're okay?"

"Ummm, yes, ma'am. I'm okay." Patrick quickly pulled his legs out of the elevator just as the doors began to close.

Once he was on his feet, he brushed his pants and shirt off. Patrick picked his gown up off the floor and tossed it over his shoulder. His cap had landed a few feet away from the exit. Marisa and her mother were already out the door and heading down the sidewalk to the auditorium. He swiped up his cap and ran for the door.

"Hey!" Patrick yelled to get Marisa's attention. "Just so you know, it *did* hurt! You could have asked me if I was okay like your mom did."

She waved him off.

"Oh, now you're going to shoo me off. That's a great way to treat your class Valedictorian."

Marisa kept walking without looking back. She and her mother headed up the auditorium stairs and disappeared inside the building.

Patrick was not far behind.

Marisa made it just in time for the faculty and student line up.

"I'm so proud of you, Rissa." Her mother said over the rising music in the auditorium.

"Thanks, Mom!" Marisa looked back at her mother as the music queued the graduates. In the distance she could see her father as he seemingly panned the graduates to find her. "Dad! Dad!" She waved her cap frantically in the air as she tried to get her father's attention. "Daddy!"

Her father finally spotted her waving hand, giving her a smile as he waved back.

"You'd better get to walking." A masculine voice came from behind where Marisa stood.

She turned toward the commanding voice. Patrick stood there motioning to the empty space in line with his hand. The graduation music started and the students began their descent down the long walk to the school's auditorium, and to the floor.

Three sections of chairs lined the auditorium floor. The graduates peeled from one filled row to the next as the thunderous sound of the music gave credence to the swinging tassels and black robes. The spectators cheered and clapped during the descent of the graduates.

One graduate after another entered the auditorium until the seats were completely filled. Some of the students peered into the crowd in hopes of getting a glimpse of family members who were there to celebrate their success. Fans with faces of graduates waved in the air.

Marisa turned to where she last saw her mother and father. Catching a quick peek at her mother, she noticed her father was nowhere in sight. Her eyes panned as much as she could until the voice of the Director of Academics began to echo through the auditorium.

Three hundred and four students sat at attention, anxiously waiting for their names to be called so they could take the stage. Finally, they would receive their hard-earned degrees from the hands of the faculty.

They would shake their hands one final time before exiting the doors for what would be their last time as students.

"Brianna Anais!"

It had begun. The name of the first graduate had been announced. The crowd held their applauses as was instructed by the class president. One by one the students walked up the stairs to receive their diplomas and down the other side. A sense of pride and accomplishment could be felt in the air with each name that was called.

Marisa rubbed her hands nervously together.

"A bit anxious, are we?" Patrick's voice echoed from the row behind her.

"What do you think? Aren't you?" she asked.

"Naw, piece of cake," he said with a cocky yet nervousness in his voice.

"Un-huh," she murmured with a slight chuckle as she sensed his nervousness, too.

At long last, she heard her name as it rang out over the auditorium. "Marisa Valerie Webb!"

She smiled as she walked up the stairs toward the awaiting diploma. Shaking with one hand and receiving with the other, she continued across the stage waving her diploma in her hand. The long, hard work she had put into earning her marketing degree was finally being realized.

Marisa rounded the seats back to where she was sitting. She looked again to where her mother stood, but her father was, still, nowhere to be found.

I won't let anything ruin this moment for me. Not even my father, she thought to herself.

Patrick, following a few students behind, tried not to show how nervous and excited he was. Climbing the stairs, he stumbled. The crowd gasped as he managed to regain his balance. He raised his hands in the air as to signal to the crowd that everything was alright. The crowd roared as Patrick made his way across the stage.

Finally back at his seat, Marisa turned toward him. "Wow! What an attention whore you are," she said.

"Oh, are you jealous?" he jokingly asked.

"What, of a tumbling clown? Not in your best dreams," She smiled sheepishly as she turned back to face the front.

Soon the last student made their descent from the stage and back to their seat.

"It gives me great pleasure to present to you the awesome Tillis University graduates of the year of our Lord, two-thousand seventeen!" the Head Master announced as the students moved their tassels from one side to the other. The audience gave a thunderous applause.

Piercing whistles also came from the crowd as the students started their ascent back up the auditorium stairs and out the door. Once outside the students flung their caps into the air as they laughed and hugged each other.

Spotting her mother in the crowd, Marisa ran down the stairs of the outside auditorium towards her.

"Oh! I'm sorry!" Marisa said to the person she had run into.

The tall figure turned around. It was Matt, Patrick's best friend. They had roomed together the whole time they were at Tillis University.

"Well, what's up, Lil' Lady," he said. His voice was husky and echoed like the voice of a radio announcer.

"I'm sorry," she said again. "I was just trying to get over there to my mother."

"Oh, no problem. I'm a big dude. Don't want cha' hurting yourself now."

"Oh," Marisa said sheepishly. "I'm okay." She brushed her hair back from the side of her face.

"So, are you coming to the graduation dance tonight?" he asked, inquisitively.

"Um, I don't know. My parents and I are going out to dinner."

"Awww," Matt said. "Party don't start until really late. You should come."

"Um, okay, I might," she said as she slowly walked away.

Matt smiled. "Well, I'll be looking for ya."

"Sure thing," Marisa said as she turned towards her mother waiting with out-stretched arms.

She embraced her mother as her eyes panned back to where Matt stood. There she saw Patrick standing as well. They both looked towards her, smiling a secret smile that made Marisa feel as if they were discussing her.

"Marisa, you ready, honey?" Her mother asked. "I've decided we are going to go to Papino's."

"Sounds great, Mom," she said as she looked around the crowd. "Where's Dad?" she asked her mother.

"Well, honey," her mother hesitated.

"Where's Dad, Mom?" she asked again. The tone of her voice began to ascend in a whine.

"Baby, he had a very important meeting and he had to leave early."

Angrily, Marisa grabbed her cell phone from her purse. Dialing her father's phone number, she folded one hand under her arm as the other hand held the phone close to her ear.

"Now, honey, it's no reason to get upset," her mother said as she rubbed her shoulder in an effort to comfort her. Tears filled Marisa's eyes as the phone began to ring. After several rings, her father's voicemail came on. She slammed the phone shut.

"How could he, Mom?" she asked her mother. "This is my college graduation!" She began to cry.

Her mother held her close. "Honey, he said he'd join us there."

"Mommy, I've decided I'm going to the graduation dance tonight instead. Is it okay if we skipped dinner?"

"Well, I wanted us to spend some time together," her mother said.

"I know, Mom. Maybe tomorrow. I'm going back to the dorm to change. I will see you tomorrow," she kissed her mom on the cheek. "Love you, Mom."

"Love you too, sweetheart."

Marisa walked down the sidewalk towards her dormitory. The night was cool and the stars lit up the sky. The moon illuminated the walkway as she followed the lightened path.

"Hey! Hey!"

Marisa turned to see whose voice it was. Waving his hand in the air, Matt stood on the outside perimeter of the water fountain that stood in front of the auditorium.

"So...you coming?" he asked.

"Yes! Yes!" Marisa said as she turned in his direction. She noticed Patrick standing only a few feet away. His cap still on his head with his gown over his shoulder. He was engaged in what seemed to be a deep conversation with Melinda—a five-foot three natural-haired African-American girl. Marisa remembered her from their French class but never became acquainted with her.

Raising her voice a little louder, "Yes! I'm coming to the dance. I wouldn't miss it for the world," she said as she peered to the side to see if Patrick was listening.

He seemed impassive to what they were discussing, and continued his conversation with Melinda.

"Well, see you there!" Matt waved at her as she turned and began, again, to slowly walk toward the co-ed building in the distance.

Soon Marisa arrived at the dorm. Still angry and drifting in her thoughts of the evening, she didn't notice the footsteps in the distance. The sound became faster as she came closer to the door.

A car's horn blew loudly as it sped by with a car full of graduates. She was startled from the sudden outburst of the sound, and watched as the car disappeared in the distance. Gathering her bearings, Marisa continued towards the entrance of the co-ed dorm she had come to call home.

Still, she didn't notice the footsteps that were gaining on her. She reached for the access card buried in the bottom of her purse, the darkness hampering her vision.

"Ouch!" she said, recoiling her hand quickly.

Her index finger had received a small cut from something inside. She had forgotten about the small box cutter she had dropped in her purse earlier that day.

"Geez!" Luckily, she had only pricked her finger just enough to draw blood.

It was at this moment, when Marisa began to raise her finger to her mouth that she heard the footsteps following so closely behind, now within arms reach of her. A hand slowly stretched out towards her as she continued raising her finger. From out of the shadows the hand landed on her shoulder. She screamed as she turned frantically in fear.

"Waaiittt! Hold on there, Lil' Lady." A voice said from the darkness. Slowly, a tall muscular figure moved into the light that faintly reflected from the dorm hallway. It was Matt.

"You screaming like you've just woke up and found out you flunked college, girl."

Marisa grabbed her chest as if to cover her heart. "Matt!" she yelled. "What the hell?! You scared the bejesus out of me."

He laughed though, then apologized. "Well, I'm sorry, little lady."

"What are you doing here?" she asked as she searched for her key card again. "Thought you were going to the graduation party?"

Matt folded his arms as he rested against the side of the doorway entrance. "I am. I saw you walking off and thought I would come and keep you company."

"Keep me company?" Marisa asked.

"Yeah," he said with a chuckle. "You shouldn't be walking by yourself in the dark."

"Oh, well, thanks, Matt. But as you are aware, I've walked that sidewalk in the dark for the past four years," Marisa said jokingly as she continued to suck on the cut on her finger.

"I know," he said as he raised up from leaning on the wall.

The light from the dorm hallway created an ominous glare on Matt's face that made Marisa nervous. She pulled her key from her purse. "Well, I'd better get going," she said as she swiped her door-key card. The light clicked to green on the panel and the door unlocked.

Matt pulled it open to allow her to walk in. "Alright, Lil' Lady," he said as he continued to hold the door.

Marisa headed down the hallway toward the elevator. She peeked back to see Matt still watching her, the light casting that ominous shadow on his face.

She hurried to the elevator. Once inside, she turned toward the elevator door. Matt was no longer standing at the end of the hall. She gave a sigh of relief, and pushed the button for the third floor.

The door opened and she stepped out onto the floor she had walked down so many times before. She stood there for a brief moment and looked toward the end of the hallway. Thoughts of her first year at Tillis University ran through her mind. It seemed strange that after calling this home for so many years that she would be leaving it tomorrow.

As Marisa opened the door of her room, she turned immediately to look behind her thinking she had heard footsteps. Suddenly, another door opened just down the hall. Two students emerged laughing as they walked towards the elevator. Marisa smiled as the students passed by.

"Coming to the dance?" one of the students asked.

"Yeah, I'll be there. Wouldn't miss it for the world."

The students chuckled as one gave her a thumbs up. "Well, see you there." They entered the elevator, then waved as the doors closed.

Marisa waved back as she walked inside her dorm closing the door behind her. She turned on her favorite radio channel to keep her company while she dressed. The space was full of boxes, suitcases and trunks. Clothes were laid out across the bed and the arms of the sofa.

"Now, where did I put those jeans?" she said out loud as she pulled one pile of clothes from the bed and searched through them.

The clutter of half folded clothes, and books, thwarted her search attempts. Finally, she pulled a top from the pile. "Oh! I can wear this with my jeans...if I can ever find them," she said loudly to herself.

Marisa stood there for a minute trying to remember where she had packed the jeans. She snapped her finger as she ran to the bathroom. There hanging across the striped white and gold shower curtain was a dark pair of blue skinny jeans. They were ripped at the knees and thighs on either side and tapered down to the ankles.

She smiled. "There you are," as if she were having a two-way conversation with them. She grabbed a pair of gold Jimmy Cho pumps from the mountain of shoe boxes lining her closet.

Heading back towards one of the small twin beds, she began to change her clothes as quickly as she could. Just as she sat down on the bed, there was a knock at the door. Puzzled as to who it could be, Marisa walked toward it. "Who is it?" she asked.

But there was no answer. Slowly, she opened the door wider but no one was there. She looked down one end of the hall and then toward the elevator. The elevator door was just closing. She managed to recognize one of the faces on the elevator. It was Tia—a girl from the school's cheerleading team. She was fairly sure the other person was the girl's boyfriend. Marisa peered again to the other end of the hallway but there was no one in sight.

Confused, she closed the door. "Humph," she said to herself. *Guess they must have hit the door while they were walking past.* She grabbed her shoes and jeans and headed for the bathroom. When she pulled the shower curtain back to cut the water on, she heard a sound. She didn't move a muscle as she strained her ear to hear.

"Hello?" Marisa called out. "Hello?" she repeated, yet again there was no answer.

All of a sudden the lights went out in the apartment. Now she was nervous.

"Hello?" she yelled. "Who's out there?"

But there was still no answer.

She had forgotten to lock the door behind her. "Who's there!" Marisa cried out nervously.

She grabbed the handle of the bathroom door when the force of someone on the other side suddenly pushed the door hard enough to knock her back. Losing her balance, she bumped her head on the bathtub.

Dazed, she could only make out the silhouette of a tall muscular figure by the light shining through the window. She could feel her clothes being ripped from her body as the tall blurred figure lifted her up off the floor, and carried her to the next room.

Marisa smelled the strong scent of a woodsy cologne on her assailant's body. Unable to stop, tears flowed down either side of her face as the light grew dimmer and dimmer.

2
The Coldness Creeps In

The next morning sunlight slowly pierced through the curtains of Marisa's small room. The warmth of the rays gently touched her face as she laid deathly quiet. She could hear the sound of a car as it slowly moved down the campus streets. Echoing from a weeping willow tree that stood by the window, she listened to the same birds she had heard so many times chirping in the distance.

Today, none of it seemed as beautiful as before. A tear slowly made its way down the left side of her cheek as she struggled to quiet her mind. With a tightly clinched fist, Marisa pounded her fist on the wall above her head.

Finally, she covered her face with her hands, and wept bitterly until the tears that streamed down her face dampened her hair. Suddenly, she stopped crying. It was as if something snapped in her head and her emotions were turned off.

Slowly, she raised from the bed. The bump on her head—and the now blackening bruises on her arms and legs—became the harsh reality that what she had experienced was not a dream. The thoughts rushed back through her mind and swirled around inside her head like a horrid nightmare.

She shut her eyes tightly and took a deep breath. Bracing either hand on the bed, Marisa found the strength to push herself up and make her way to the bathroom.

Numbly, she pulled the shower curtain back as she reached for the knob. Fighting back her thoughts, she again was startled by another knock at her door. Marisa looked toward the bathroom door as fear gripped her, almost paralyzing her. She picked up a box cutter lying on the shelf of the linen closet. Shaking, she stared at the door. The room felt as if it was spinning while she stumbled backwards.

Her foot touched the base of the bathtub. Holding the box cutter in one hand, she slowly reached with her other hand to feel the edge of the bathtub. Then the second knock came.

"Marisa! Marisa!"

She recognized the voice. It was Caroline, the girl across the hall.

"Marisa!" The voice called out again.

But she sat quietly, hoping the girl would go away. A few minutes passed before she realized the knocking had stopped. Raising from the side of the tub, she turned on the shower head, undressed and stepped inside.

Submerging her head under the warm, soft rain of water, she closed her eyes as it traveled down her bruised body. She looked up and grabbed the soft loofa sponge from around the shower head and lathered herself from head to toe.

After what seemed like hours, she finally emerged from the shower and reached for her bathrobe. The soft fluff of the robe gave her a sense of comfort as she wrapped it around her dampened body. She grabbed a towel from the closet and slowly wrapped her dripping wet hair.

Marisa made her way to the kitchen. Hitting the button on the coffee pot, she stood there quietly. The aroma from the brewing coffee filled the small galley-type kitchen. She had begun to pour herself a cup of coffee when another knock came at the door. Again she hesitated, then slowly walked toward it.

"Marisa!"

The voice that echoed from the other side of the door was her mother's. She quickly grabbed the door knob and opened it, making her mother jump from the suddenness.

"Oh! I was about to leave. I thought you weren't..."

Marisa grabbed her mother and hugged her tightly.

Surprised, she slowly put her arms around her, confused. "Honey, are you okay?!"

Marisa simply held onto her without saying a word. After a while, she regained her composure. Wiping tears from her eyes, she hurried back to the kitchen, knowing her mother would be following close behind.

"Mom, you want a cup of coffee?"

"Um, yes. Sure, dear."

Marisa poured another cup of coffee.

"Honey, is everything okay?"

"Yes, sure." Her hands were shaking when she handed her mother the cup. "I was just thinking how I'd be flying off to Europe soon and how much I'm going to miss you."

"Aww, sweetheart. We're going to miss you, too." Her mother hugged her again. "This is an opportunity of a lifetime for you. Think about all you will learn from being in another country with different cultural ideas and ways of living."

"Yes, it is!" Marisa sipped her coffee. "So, where's Dad? In California again?"

"Well, honey, he said he was so sorry he didn't get to stay to your graduation but he would make it up to you."

Marisa listened to her mother make excuses for her father, but now, it didn't really seem to matter as much anymore. She and her mother talked for a while, and as the evening continued on her mother stood up from the couch.

"Well, honey, I should get going," she said, walking to the kitchen to place her coffee cup in the sink.

"Okay," Marisa mumbled, following her to the door.

"We'll be back to pick you up for the airport tomorrow."

"Alright, Mom."

"Don't you forget," her mother cautioned, playfully.

"No, Mom, that is not something I would forget. Quite frankly the sooner I leave, the better."

Her mother, sensing something was wrong, looked back at her as they walked toward the door. "Are you sure you're okay, honey?" she said as she took Marisa's hand and gently caressed it.

"Yes, Mom. I'm good. Just tired from all the excitement on yesterday."

She knew she couldn't tell her mother what had happened just last night. It was too painful and she just wanted to forget it.

"Well, okay. Would you tell me if something *was* wrong?" her mother said as she hugged her.

"Sure, Mom. Sure."

Her mother headed down the hallway toward the elevator. Once inside, she turned and waved. Marisa leaned on the entrance of the doorway and waved back.

The sun's rays bounced off of the elevator doors, slightly obscuring her mother's frame from her sight as they slowly closed.

Standing there staring at the elevator, she was startled suddenly by the voices that came from behind her. She quickly turned to see two male students moving furniture from their dorm room. Stepping back inside, she backed away from the door, staring wide-eyed at the knob when suddenly there was a knock.

Marisa gasped as she dropped the cup in her hand. Hot coffee spilled onto her feet as the cup shattered into pieces on the floor. She stood paralyzed, her heart racing inside her chest. Looking around for anything she could grab to protect herself, the knock came again.

"Who's there?!" Marisa yelled. But there was no answer. "Who's there?!" This time her tone demanding the person on the other side answer her.

"It's me, girl, open up!"

"Me who?!"

"Tiffany, your best friend! Remember me?! The tall black girl with the natural hair, small derrière and cute face, remember?"

Feeling a bit faint from fear, Marisa placed her hand on her forehead. With memories fresh in her mind and bruises visible on various parts of her body, she slowly walked towards the door. As she reached for the door knob, Tiffany yelled again.

"Girl, what's taking you so long? You got a man up in there? Open up!" Tiffany continued to knock.

When she opened the door, Tiffany peered around Marisa's shoulder as she pushed the door wider.

"Girl, what's wrong with you...and why weren't you at the party last night? It was *crazy*."

Marisa turned away, moving out of the way as her friend closed the door behind her.

"Lock the door, Tiffany."

"Huh?"

"I said lock the door!"

Tiffany locked the door. "Wow! You're mighty grumpy. I thought you said you were coming to the party. It was—"

"Something came up," she said, interrupting Tiffany's report from the senior graduation party.

"Something came up?!" Tiffany put her hands on her hips. "Something like what?"

Unprepared to answer, Marisa shrugged her shoulders.

"Ooo, girl you *did* have a man up in her." Tiffany grabbed her arm.

Marisa flinched in pain. Suddenly unable to contain her emotions, she burst into tears.

"Oh my God, Marisa, what's wrong?! What's wrong?"

But she only fell to her knees as she cried profusely, burying her face in her hands. Tiffany fell to her knees beside her. Hugging her, she began to gently rock back and forth as she brushed her hair from her face...

The next morning, Tiffany was awakened by noises coming from the small kitchen. Marisa had shared with her what happened last night. She sat up and looked towards the kitchen, taking a deep breath before walking inside.

"Hey, girl." Tiffany said as she gently brushed Marisa's hair back. "How you doing?"

Her eyes were red and swollen from crying. "I'm okay, Tiffany. Thanks for staying with me last night. I don't know if I could have stayed by myself."

"You know I got you, girl. So," she hesitated for a minute. "Are you going to report this to the police?"

Marisa stood there holding the coffee pot under the running water, unmoving for a moment. "No, Tiffany! I Just want to forget the whole thing ever happened!" Marisa placed the carafe on the coffee maker.

"But, Marisa...someone violated you. They came in this dorm and—"

"I'm not reporting this!" She blurted out all of a sudden. "I—I should have locked the door. I should have locked the *damn door!*" She began crying again.

"Okay, okay!" Tiffany embraced her. "Let's just...um. Let's just make some coffee and scramble some eggs. Girl, you know ain't nothing like eggs, coffee..." Just then the bread popped up from inside the toaster and Tiffany pulled it out. "...and a burnt piece of toast in the morning."

Marisa turned around to see her friend holding up the charred piece of bread. They looked at each other and burst into laughter. After breakfast Tiffany helped her finish packing for the airport.

"Mom and Dad will be here soon," Marisa said as she looked up.

"So what time does your flight leave?" She was now sitting on top of a suitcase by the door.

"Well, I have to be there no later than eleven forty-five. 'Course the flight doesn't leave until one o'clock. You know how flying international can be."

Tiffany nodded her head in agreement. "Sure do. Remember that time we were going to the *Down Under* and I thought I had left my passport?" She was now standing with her right hand on her hip.

Marisa smiled as she looked up at her. "Yeah, I will never forget that moment. You had put it in your bra because you didn't want to forget it. When you finally remembered...you had to pull it out in front of all those people."

Tiffany and Marisa laughed.

A knock sounded so suddenly on the door that they stopped instantly and stared at each other.

"Marisa, honey. It's Mom."

"Oh my goodness! I'm not done!" Marisa said as she picked up the pace, packing as quickly as she could.

"Marisa!"

The tiny voice called out again from the other side of the door. Tiffany slowly opened it as she peeped outside.

"Mrs. Webb, is that you?"

Marisa's mother looked confused. Realizing it was Tiffany, they both laughed and hugged one another.

"Well, Tiffany! How are you, dear?"

"I'm doing well, Mrs. Webb."

Smiling, Marisa watched them as she continued packing. Mrs. Webb walked over and hugged her.

"Hello, honey."

"Hi, Mom."

Her mother pulled a cloth from her purse. "Well, our girl is headed off to Europe," she said as she began to tear up.

"Aw, Mrs. Webb. Your little girl will be just fine," Tiffany said as she walked over to embrace her. "You'll miss your mom, too. Won't you, Marisa?" Tiffany beckoned her to join them in a group hug.

"Of course I will. Mom, don't you worry, okay? I will be just fine." Marisa looked at Tiffany as they both embraced her mother. "I will be just fine."

Marisa finally arrived at the Kennedy Airport. Her flight to Europe would be boarding within the next hour. She watched as the planes taxied on and off the runway.

Suddenly, she drifted off in her thoughts. Images of the night after graduation began to flash through her mind. Like a sharp knife piercing into her head she could hear his breathing, feel the painful grip of his hand, and smell the engulfing scent of his wood-scented cologne.

She shut her eyes as if to squeeze out the paralyzing images from her brain. Then...a familiar voice greeted her from behind.

"Well, howdy there, little lady."

Startled, Marisa looked up. Her vision was obscured by the bright recess lighting of the airport. She could make out a tall, muscular figure of a man.

As he stood there next to her seat Marisa felt almost transfixed. The tall figure moved around into the isle of the seats, blocking out the blinding lights.

It was Matt.

He wore a pair of dark blue jeans and a white pullover collared shirt. His dark brown leather dress shoes seemed freshly polished. A feeling of anxiety engulfed her entire being.

"What are you doing here?!" she said, her anxiety increasing. The palms of her hands became sweaty as she moved closer to the other side of the chair.

"Whoa, whoa, little lady. I'm doing the same thing you're doing—I'm catching a flight."

He moved slightly and the recess light overhead blinded her again as she tried to focus in on his face.

"Catching a flight?"

"Yep! I'm going to Paris, then I'm gone hop on over to Europe for a job interview."

Marisa looked over at the ticket desk.

"Flight 19647 will be boarding in five minutes." The voice of the hostess echoed across the intercom.

Feeling panicked, she grabbed her purse and hurried towards the gate. Frantically, she searched for her first-class boarding pass.

"I'm sorry, miss, you will have to step to the side until you locate your boarding pass."

Just then Marisa pulled the ticket from her purse. "Here. Here it is."

"Thank you, ma'am." The attendant reached for the ticket. "Enjoy your flight."

Marisa hurried onto the plane. Matt stood in the distance watching as she walked down the corridor to board. She placed her carry-on in the above compartment. Visibly shaken, she tried to push the overhead door shut but soon collapsed in her seat. She placed her hands over her face to fight back the tears she felt swelling in her eyes. She was suddenly aware of a presence standing over her, but it was only another passenger putting their luggage in the compartment overhead. Relief flooded her when, finally, the voice of the pilot sounded over the intercom. They were getting ready to taxi onto the runway.

Thank God I'm getting away from this awful city, she thought as she leaned her head back and reclined her seat.

She let the faint roar of the engines calm her while she gazed out the small window. The sun played peek-a-boo behind the white floating clouds. She smiled as she felt the sun rays hit her face through the glass. Exhausted, she drifted off. She imagined herself lying on the cloud without a care in the world. All the events of the past few days seemed to drift away with each passing cloud.

"Hello. Thank you for flying with us. I hope you're enjoying your flight."

Marisa turned to see one of the flight stewardesses standing at her seat.

"Would you like to order dinner?"

"Oh, um, no thank you." Marisa smiled as she looked up at the woman. "Could you tell me about what time we will be arriving in London?"

"If you will give me a moment I can definitely get you the approximate time."

Marisa smiled and nodded her head. Soon the stewardess returned.

"We should arrive in London within the next six hours."

"Thank you."

Lying back once again, the humming of the plane's engines and the dull chatter of the other passengers seemed to give her a sense of calm and safety. The noise slowly faded into the background as she drifted off into sleep.

"Ladies and Gentlemen, we will be landing at the London City Airport here in about fifteen minutes," the pilot's muzzled voice streamed over the intercom.

Marisa slowly opened her eyes to a dark starry sky. Raising her seat from the inclined position, she realized she had slept through much of the flight. She leaned her head on the small window, gazing at the twinkling starlit night. She could faintly make out the glittering lights below.

In the distance a star shot aimlessly across the sky. She thought of how her father used to tell her to make a wish whenever she saw a shooting star. Marisa closed her eyes. Clasping one arm across her chest, she crossed her fingers and closed her eyes. Quietly, she whispered her wish, then slowly opened her eyes.

The plane began its descent. In the distance, glowing in the night like a beacon of hope, stood the tower known as Big Ben among all the other lights surrounding it. The view was more than Marisa had imagined. She listened as the plane's wheels emerged from their hiding place the last several hours. She watched the wings of the plane shift positions as the whistling of the wind rushed through, slowing the aircraft for landing.

The captain's voice came across the intercom: *"Ladies and Gentlemen, you have reached your final destination. Thank you for flying with us."*

They had finally landed. Marisa grabbed her overhead luggage and headed for the exit.

"Thank you flying with us, ma'am. We hope you enjoyed your flight," the attendant said, smiling as she stood near the door of the cockpit.

Marisa smiled. "I did. Thank you very much."

She walked out the airplane door. Tired from the near fifteen-hour flight, she decided to bunk out at the nearest hotel for the night.

The next morning Marisa woke to the faint sounds of airplanes and car engines. The day had gotten started without her. She laid there for a moment just listening to the sounds. All of a sudden there was a knock at the door.

Marisa sat up.

She waited for a moment, to see if the knock was at *her* door. And then it came again.

Maybe it's the maid, she thought. She looked at the clock. *It was only seven o'clock in the morning. It can't be the maid,* she thought again.

Marisa moved slowly towards the edge of the bed. She wasn't expecting anyone and no one knew she was at this hotel. The third knock came. She quietly walked to the window, peeping out to see who was there. The angle of the hotel room made it impossible for her to see the doorway. She walked to the door, placing her hand on the knob.

"Who is it?"

A muffled voice came from the other side.

"Who?!" She asked again.

The voice spoke again, but again, it was too soft for her to understand.

Finally, she mustered up enough courage to open the door. Fear gripped her as flashes of the night of the rape flooded her thoughts at that moment. Slowly she opened the door, wider and wider. She couldn't see anyone.

Maybe there were kids playing. But three times? she thought.

She opened the door wider when all of a sudden the door was whisked opened out of Marisa's hand. She gasped!

"Surprise!" A voice yelled as the door swung open. "Girl! You're in London! What are you doing sleeping?"

Marisa looked with disbelief.

"Tiffany?! OMG! When did you get here?! How did you? How did you know I was even here at this hotel?!"

"Girl...really?" she said looking at Marisa as if dumbfounded that she would ask that question. "How long have we been friends?"

"Um, since middle school." Marisa shrugged her shoulders.

"Who knew that you slept with drawls on your head because you thought it made your hair shine?"

"Really, Tiffany?"

"Who?" she asked again as Marisa sighed.

"You, Tiffany."

"See, I know you girl! It's like I'm the yin to your yang! The Alpha to your Omega, the—"

Marisa interrupted. "Yeah, yeah, I get it! Get over here." She grabbed her. "Girl, I'm so glad to see you."

"Aww, me too," she replied as she smiled and hugged Marisa back. Then she pulled away suddenly. "So, enough of that hugging stuff, girl. Where's the food? I'm hungry."

"You're always hungry," Marisa chuckled. "Remember when we were in our science class and your stomach growled so loud Professor Crate turned from the board and looked?"

Tiffany laughed. "He said, 'Someone's intestines are working overtime today'," both girls said in unison.

After a moment of bated silence, they fell back on the bed laughing hysterically. They laid there for a while as their laughing whittled down to silence. They stared at the ceiling for a moment. The quiet humming of the ceiling fan coupled with the faint sounds of airplane engines in the distance brought a sense of calm to the room.

"So," Tiffany said softly, but with caution in her voice. "How are you, Rissa?"

For a minute there was no reply. Only silence. Marisa turned her face toward her.

"I'm good," she said somberly. "I take one day at a time, you know?"

"Did you—" Tiffany stopped in mid-sentence. "You know what, I'm not here to talk about that. My feet hurt, I have jet lag, and—" Just then, her stomach growled. She grabbed her stomach as she looked up, "—I'm hungry."

The girls burst into laughter again as they raised from the bed. They headed out the door after Marisa got dressed.

"Come on, girl. You and your intestines," she said shaking her head.

Hailing a cab, Marisa and Tiffany jumped in just as the rain began to fall.

"Where to, ladies?"

Marisa looked over at Tiffany.

"We'd like to go somewhere where they serve breakfast."

Tiffany leaned up towards the driver. "Do you know of any good places?"

The cab driver slowly turned to look at her. With a scrubby beard the man looked to be in his fifties. His voice was deep with a strong accent. He wore a plaid red and black shirt. A green tee could be seen from the top of the shirt, where a broken black button held the shirt together. His hat, a bit tattered, was pulled down just above his thick salt and peppered brows.

"You want restaurant, no?"

Leaning back in her seat, she said, "Uh, Yes. Restaurant." Her eyes widened as her hand moved towards the door handle.

The driver's face lit up as he laughed out loud. "I know a good one. I will take you there."

Marisa and Tiffany glared at each other as he put the car in gear and headed down the street. Tiffany leaned over, still eyeing the driver. "We're gonna die!" They both chuckled as the car continued down the road.

After about fifteen minutes, the cabbie pulled up to an orange building. The boards, intentionally distressed, appeared worn and old. Brown blinds were neatly pulled up to the top of the window. An awning hung out over the sidewalk. Three tables were nestled under the awning's shade. And a single small but welcoming yellow and white floral arrangement sat in the middle of each table.

Marisa's eyes panned upward to the white writing that ran across the front of the building: *Club des petits déjeuners.*

"Breakfast Club," Marisa read out loud as she turned towards Tiffany. Suddenly Marisa's car door swung open. Startled, she turned to see Tiffany standing on the sidewalk.

"What is it with you and these doors lately? Girl, I told you I was hungry. Let's go."

Marisa grabbed her purse and opened it to pay the driver.

"Um, while you were daydreaming, Miss Thang, I paid the man and tipped him. Let's go!" Standing in front of the restaurant, Tiffany looked at the facing of the building. "Well, this doesn't look all fancy but I do hope the food is good." She grabbed the door handle and beckoned Marisa to step inside.

They seated themselves in a corner of the restaurant. The table was flush against a gray brick wall. A painting of purple grapes and a string of green vines stretched from one end of the wall to the other. The table for two was covered with a red and white checkered table cloth. Just then, a tall, dark-haired waiter came from behind two doubled doors and stood at the middle of their table.

He wore a white apron that wrapped snugly around his waist. A slightly hairy wrist peeped barely from underneath a white long sleeved shirt. The cuffs had been rolled up just above his wrists. Smiling warmly, he greeted the girls.

"Good morning, mademoiselles. What will you ladies be ordering this morning?"

"Coffee to start, please."

"And you, mademoiselle?"

Marisa looked up from her menu when she didn't hear Tiffany answer. "Tiff, Tiff…" she gently kicked her leg under the table.

"Huh?"

"The gentleman asked a question."

"Oh, my apologies. What was your question again?" The waiter chuckled. "What can I get you today?"

"Oh, I'll have what she said."

"Um, coffee?" The waiter asked.

"Yes, yes…coffee."

"Okay. Be right back."

The waiter walked off as Tiffany turned around watching him disappear behind two swinging silver doors. "Lord have mercy!" she said, turning back towards Marisa who was now shaking her head.

"Got your mind off food for a minute, did he?" she smiled.

"Honey, I can work with that. A little skinny. I'd have to fatten him up just a bit. Wouldn't want to break him, you know."

Marisa placed her hands over her face. "Tiffany…" she paused for a second. "Look at the menu already."

The waiter returned with the coffee and took their orders.

"So, how's the breakfast steak?"

Tiffany looked up at Marisa. "Honey, it's soooo good. How's your chicken?"

"Well, it's not as good as Ms. Braxton's but it's good. Tiff, your mom must have a secret recipe she's not sharing with anyone for her chicken, I swear."

Tiffany chuckled. "Yeah, I don't know if she sticks her toes in it or what but it's—" she noticed a strange look on Marisa's face. Her eyes were fixed on a old bronze Victorian mirror that hung just behind Tiffany's head. Her face had suddenly turned pale as she stared in the mirror.

"Marisa. Marisa. Okay, like, you're scaring me. Do you feel okay?" She grabbed Marisa's hand. "You're shaking! What's wrong?"

"I thought I saw someone."

She turned and looked at the mirror. "What? A ghost in the mirror?"

"You can say that," Marisa said as the color began to come back to her cheeks.

"Can you be more specific?" By now, Tiffany had gone from scared to confused.

"When I..." Marisa hesitated. "...was at the airport waiting for my flight to London, I was sitting down and suddenly felt this presence behind me. When I looked up it was Matt."

"Matt? Matt from college?" her friend asked with a bit of relief.

"Yes," she said, looking her in the eyes. "He said he was coming to London as well."

"Okay..." Tiffany was now thoroughly confused.

Marisa was about to go into more detail when she was interrupted by the waiter.

"So, how are you ladies enjoying your breakfast?"

Tiffany looked up at the waiter. "Oh, it was *delish*. The steak and eggs were excellent." They looked at Marisa. Seeing that she was still a bit dazed, Tiffany answered for her. "Oh, hers was so good she's speechless."

Marisa looked up at the waiter and then back at Tiffany.

"Well, can I get you anything else?"

"No, no thank you. We appreciate everything." Tiffany smiled as she looked up at the waiter.

The girls finished off their breakfast and headed back to the hotel.

"So, are you going to finish telling me what you were about to tell me at the restaurant?" Tiffany said, squinting at Marisa.

"Well, that was all."

"That was all?" Tiffany's voice escalated. "That's all? You became as pale as a ghost, scaring the bejesus out of me and all you can say is 'that was all'?"

"Yes. So, how long are you going to stay, Tiff?"

"Oh, so you're just going to change the conversation just like that, huh?" she stared at Marisa with a look of sarcasm.

But before she could answer the cab pulled up to the hotel.

"So, again I ask, are you just going to change the conversation?"

"Yes, I am," Marisa said as she paid the driver. "It wasn't important."

Tiffany mumbled something as she rolled her eyes. "Well, I'm here for a couple of weeks."

Marisa turned to look at her, watching the girl as she lagged behind her.

"I'm going to help you look for a place. After all, I'll be moving back here in a few months," she said nonchalantly.

Marisa turned and walked back towards Tiffany.

"What?! Tiffany, are you serious?!"

"Yes, girl! I'm moving to London, too!"

Marisa hugged her as they both screamed and laughed. "Oh my gosh! You're the bestest friend I've ever had, Tiff!" She held her tightly as she continued jumping up and down.

"Yes, I am. Actually, I'm the *only* bestest friend you've ever had. Now let go. You're smothering me."

The girls chuckled as they walked onto the elevator to the second floor.

The next morning they took a cab across town. Marisa had scheduled appointments with a local realtor while she was still in the states.

Tiffany turned her whole body toward her, resting her right knee on the seat. "So, are you excited?"

"Excited about what?"

"Girl, stop playing. Are you excited about, like, all of this?" she said, waving her hands in the air, a glint of excitement in her eyes.

"Well, I am. I'm just ready to start fresh. Leave all the crazy behind me." Marisa looked over at her. "I'm glad to be getting away from my passive mother and my—" she paused suddenly.

"And your what?" Looking intensely at Marisa who turned to look out the window.

"...my dad."

Tiffany looked with surprise and confusion. "Your dad? Not you. Not *daddy's little girl*."

Marisa's tone turned angry. "You know my dad was only at my graduation for a few minutes?"

Tiffany sat quietly as she chuckled sarcastically.

"Mom said he was working late. Thing is, Tiff," she turned, looking her in the eyes. "I don't believe for one minute that he was working."

Tiffany glanced out of the front of the car then back at her. "Where do you think he was?"

Marisa's head dropped. Tiffany would be the only one she could share this information with. "I know for a fact that Daddy was having an affair."

"What?" Tiffany placed her hand on her lips as she gasped in disbelief.

"Remember when I took that trip to L.A. for the Sorority convention? Well, one evening me and some of the girls went out on the town. We wanted to relax, get a few drinks, you know, just be sociable…"

Tiffany tried not to show her anxiety. She had known Mr. Webb all of her life and had always viewed him with respect.

"We went to a couple of clubs and then to Bowshenier."

"Is that the restaurant a couple of blocks off of Rodeo?" she asked.

"Yeah, well, we were seated over in the corner off from the entrance of the door. After ordering, I headed to the ladies room and who do I see all cozy at a secluded table?" Marisa sighed. "He sat there all snuggled up and intimate with this bimbo." Her eyes filled up with tears.

Tiffany grabbed her hand in an effort to console her.

"I was so shocked. I just stood there for a second in disbelief; paralyzed in the middle of the floor. I finally came to myself and hurried back to the table. I told the girls I had an emergency and had to leave."

"Wow. Did your dad see you?"

"No, but when he got back home, I asked him how he enjoyed his dinner at Bowshenier."

Tiffany could hardly believe what she was hearing. "Oh my gosh! You did? What did he say?"

"What could he say, Tiff? He just looked at me with this dumb look on his face."

Tiffany shook her head as she leaned back in her seat. "Dang, girl. I'm so sorry," she said empathetically.

"It's no matter. I've concluded that men are selfish, lying evil bas—" Suddenly the driver advised that they would be at their destination soon. She leaned her head on the window of the car.

For the next ten miles the girls sat quietly. Marisa leaned her head against the window and watched the buildings fade in the distance, and the array of green grass lining the sides of the road. In the distance she could see a field of daffodils and chrysanthemums waving freely in meadows. Beautifully colored butterflies cascaded up into the air, circling off into the vast clear blue sky.

"It must be a wonderful feeling to be free," she said softly.

"Huh?" Tiffany turned towards her. She had been sitting quietly trying to process all that her friend had told her.

"Oh, nothing. I was just thinking out loud," she said, turning to look at Tiffany. "You know, I think I'm going to plant some yellow chrysanthemums once I find a place."

"Yellow? Why yellow?" she asked inquisitively.

"Yellow because it represents how I feel."

"How are you feeling, Marisa?" she sounded empathetic in her tone.

For a few moments she just sat quietly. She placed her hands together, and fought back the swelling of tears as they threatened to fill her eyes again. "Well, they represent sorrow. The emptiness I feel when I ask why this happened to me and there is no answer…only silence."

Tiffany placed her hand on her shoulder. "I don't know either, Rissa. What I do know is I will always be here for you. Anytime you feel you need or want to talk, I'm here."

The car soon pulled up to a building. "Here we are, ladies," the driver said.

"This must be the place." Marisa looked outside her window.

"Prunes Realty." Tiffany read out aloud. "What kind of name is that? I hope they're not full of—"

"Tiffany!" Marisa called out before the girl could finish her sentence.

"What?" she said with a bit of a smirk.

"You have absolutely no filters, do you?"

"Nope," Tiffany said as she snapped her fingers. "As a matter of fact, I just believe in keeping it all the way one hundred."

The girls chuckled as they exited the car and walked into the building. Marisa walked up to the counter just as the receptionist was finishing up a call.

"Hello, I'm here to see Glenna High, please."

"Sure thing. Let me get her." The receptionist walked down a short hallway and disappeared around the corner.

Tiffany looked around the waiting area.

"Okay," she nodded her head slightly.

Marisa turned away from the counter. "Okay, what?"

"The office. Not bad. Beautiful office foliage, dark Emperador tile, and high ceilings. And would you look at that mid-century crystal chandelier?" Tiffany gasped. "See this is the kind of building I'm going to design one day, except better."

"It is a beautiful building. The outside doesn't do the inside justice," Marisa responded. "Did you get that bid for Merckles Architects and Building Design Company?" Marisa asked.

"Actually, I got an internship there for a year and then…" Tiffany stopped and just smiled.

Marisa looked at her with curiosity. She waited for her to complete her sentence. "Stop playing, Tiffany. Then what?"

"And then…I'm coming to London. Permanently!"

They both screamed. Marisa ran over and slung her arms around her neck. They both jumped up and down so excitedly that staff members began peering from their offices to see what was happening.

"Well, can I join the party?"

The girls turned around still laughing with joy. A tall slender, well-dressed woman in her fifties, with red hair and green eyes, stood there smiling.

"Hello, I'm Glenna," the woman said, stretching out her hand.

"Oh! Hi, Ms.—" Marisa hesitated briefly, a slight awkward look came across her face. "Uh, Ms. High?"

The woman nodded her head as she smiled. "Yes."

"I'm Marisa and this is my best friend, Tiffany Braxton," she said as they shook hands.

Glenna chuckled. "I get that a lot. It can be a bit awkward saying 'hi' to Ms. High, so just call me Glenna."

They all chuckled. "Come on into my office," she said, turning around and motioning for the girls to follow.

"Your office is absolutely beautiful, Glenna."

"Thank you, Marisa," she said as they continued towards her office. "My friend, Tiffany, is an architect and graphics design major."

Tiffany smiled in agreement.

"Wow! That sounds pretty exciting."

"Yes, college was pretty exciting...I mean the classes, the classes were pretty exciting." Tiffany looked at Glenna as she pressed her lips together and widened her eyes from embarrassment.

Glenna chuckled. "It's okay, Tiffany. I was once your age, and *in* college. You girls are about, what, twenty or twenty-one?"

Marisa smiled. "I'm twenty-three."

Glenna looked at Tiffany. "And you, young lady?"

Marisa tapped her. "Oh, me? Oh, I'm twenty-two."

Tiffany had become distracted. Her eyes gazing into the office next door.

Marisa followed her line of sight to the adjacent office. There, standing at a file cabinet, was a young man about six feet tall. His black dreaded hair was neatly pulled back into a ponytail that hung to the middle of his shoulder blades. His bass-filled exotic accent was distinctly audible as he spoke on the phone.

"Oh, that's Ryan Mason," Glenna said, smiling. "He's one of our top agents here at Prunes."

Ryan sat down in his plush burgundy office chair, turning from side to side as he spoke. Suddenly he noticed he was on display. He smiled sheepishly as he continued his conversation.

"Wow!" Tiffany said slowly as she turned back towards Glenna and Marisa. "Did you guys see that?"

They both looked puzzled. "See what?"

"When he smiled...you guys didn't see the *ting* that sparkled on his teeth?"

"Ting?" Glenna asked with confusion in her voice.

"Yes, you know when people smile on TV and you see that flash of light showing how bright their smile is?"

"Um," Glenna said looking at Marisa as she placed her hand over her mouth and chuckled. "So, I've lined up a few places for you to see, Marisa. Actually one is only a few blocks down the street. That will be the first one we will go see." Glenna gathered a couple of files and stood up from her desk. "The other two are about three blocks from the night life area and will also put you closer to downtown."

"That sounds great, Glenna."

"Okay. Well, let's go."

Glenna and Marisa continued to talk as they headed for the exit. Tiffany lagged a few feet behind finding herself knocking on Ryan's door.

"Excuse me…"

Ryan looked up from reviewing some papers on his desk.

"Hi, my name is Tiffany. I couldn't help but notice all the plaques on your wall."

Ryan looked at the plaques then turned back towards Tiffany. "Hi. Um, yes, I'm very blessed, you know."

"Yes, you are," Tiffany said smiling. "Um, so I understand you're one of the company's top agents."

He smiled at her. "Yeah, that's what I'm told. I just try to carry my weight, you know. So…you ladies looking for a place?"

Tiffany stood there quietly. Ryan waved his hand in the air. "Helloooo…"

"Huh? Oh yeah, I mean, no. I mean, my best friend is. She's moving here. I will be coming back later though."

"Oh? Wow, well that's awesome," he said enthusiastically.

"Oh, what a lovely picture," she said suddenly, referring to a picture of Ryan embraced by a young woman.

Looking back at the picture, he smiled. "Yeah, that's my beautiful roommate."

"Your roommate?" her voice cracked.

"Yeah, that's the love of my life," Ryan said knowing what Tiffany was up to.

"Oh. How long have you two been together?"

"Well, about twenty-two years."

As a look of confusion came over the girl's face, Ryan began to laugh. "She's my baby sister."

A look of relief now came over her face as he continued to laugh. "My sister is attending LSDA and it's just more convenient for her to live with me.

"LSDA?" Tiffany responded inquisitively.

"Yes. London School of Dramatic Arts. It's considered the best acting school in London."

She looked back at the picture.

"It makes Mum feel better knowing she's with me. We actually took this for her. That's why we're waving. We had two copies made and sent my mum one, and I kept this one."

"Oh, okay. So, that's your sister." Tiffany said with another sigh of relief. "What's her name?"

"Her name's Indra," he said as he took the picture from the shelf.

By this time Marisa had come back down the hall. "Tiffany, Tiffany! Psst!"

Tiffany slowly leaned backward, her head just barely poking out of Ryan's door. Marisa beckoned with a wild wave of her hand.

"Come on, girl."

"Oh...um, well, it was nice talking to you. Guess I'd better go. Got apartments to see."

Ryan smiled. "Okay, hope too see you again soon."

"Yeah, me too," Tiffany said as she slowly pulled one of his business cards from the cardholder on his desk. Slowly backing out of the office Tiffany held up the card. "Well, nice meeting you, Ryan."

"Same here, Tiffany."

Marisa walked down the hall to where her friend was standing. The girl was still talking to Ryan when Marisa grabbed her arm and pulled her along.

"Bye!" Tiffany said again as she waved to him.

3
The Search for Tranquility

Glenna's car pulled up to a row of pastel-colored houses that lined the road for about two blocks. Black wrought-iron fences enclosed each unit. The paint that outlined the parking spaces looked fresh. And across the street was a park filled with a lot of people, most of them had pets running to and fro.

"Wow, this seems to be a pretty family-oriented area, Glenna," Marisa said as she opened the car door. She looked around the area for a few moments. "So, what do you think, Tiffany?" she said, gazing back into the car.

Tiffany got out, taking a curious look over at the dog park. "It seems kind of busy." She closed the door just as a vehicle sped by. Turning to look at her friend with raised brows, Marisa only shrugged her shoulders.

"Well, ladies, let's take a look inside." The gate that enclosed the apartment creaked as Glenna pushed it open. "This is a one bedroom, one bath," she said as she unlocked the door. "Your bedroom and bath are upstairs. You have, of course, your living room and kitchen over there—" Just as Glenna was walking through a small French door, there was a loud thump. She and Marisa turned to see what it was.

Tiffany was stooped down picking up something from the floor. As she stood up she noticed both of them staring. "What?" she said. Slowly she pulled a round object from behind her back. "I didn't break it. I just put my hand on the staircase and this piece fell off."

Marisa looked back at Glenna.

"It's an old apartment, but that's cosmetic and can be fixed."

"Well, I think it has lots of character," Marisa said looking at Tiffany.

Glenna smiled, and turned to continue the tour. Tiffany placed the broken piece back on the end of the staircase as she mouthed the word *no* to Marisa and pointed back to the stairs. Marisa placed her hand over her mouth to muzzle the sound of laughter as the ball fell again. They continued from the small living room to the kitchen.

"This has a pretty odd shape," Marisa said as she walked to a corner that angled into an L-shape.

"Yes, well, this little area could be used as a breakfast nook."

"Yes, I can see that," she replied as she stood there with her hand on her cheek.

Tiffany's eyes widened as she looked at the area.

"Okay, let's head upstairs."

She pulled Marisa's arm. "Girl, this is a death trap!"

"Shhh," Marisa said as she placed her hand over Tiffany's mouth.

The tour of the upstairs revealed a small closet and an even smaller bathroom. "Wow, this is really small."

Glenna nodded at Marisa. "Yes, I thought this would be pretty nice for a starter apartment. You could do a six months lease. Then as you get to know the area you can decide if you want to continue here, or elsewhere," she said as they walked from the kitchen back to the entrance.

"That's a good idea. Honestly, I'm not really feeling this one, Glenna."

"Well, I have a few more for you to see."

"Okay, great!"

Just as they were getting into the car a dog and his owner crossed the street. Tiffany opened the door when suddenly the dog began to bark. She noticed that the owner was having a difficult time managing the animal. Hurrying into the car, she locked the door behind her. Marisa laughed as she got in, and laughed even more when Tiffany pushed her in the shoulder.

"That's not funny, girl."

Marisa turned around and looked at her. "Um, yes it was." They both laughed as they drove off to view two more apartments.

After looking at two additional apartments, Marisa decided they were farther away than what she'd liked.

"Well, we can look again tomorrow," Glenna said as they headed back to the office. "I will look at some that are a bit closer to town and determine if they are in your price point. We will get together to take a look at those."

"Awesome," Marisa said as they all got out of the car.

Glenna shook their hands and headed back towards the office building. Just as she reached for the door, Ryan was on his way out.

"Hi, Glenna. How did it go?"

She stopped for a moment as Ryan held the door. "Well, we didn't find anything today, but I'm sure we will."

He smiled. "Oh, absolutely. Well, I'm out. Have a great evening, Glenna."

"You, too, Ryan. Thank you," she said and walked on into the building.

The girls chatted about the apartments as they looked to hail a cab. Ryan's distinctive voice caught Tiffany's attention. Turning around, she realized he was walking in their direction.

"Well, ladies, how did it go?"

Tiffany acted as if she was surprised to see him. "Oh...hi, Ryan. Um, We saw some really nice places," she blurted out before Marisa could respond.

"Yes, I will be looking again tomorrow with the assistance of my friend Tiffany."

Tiffany smiled wryly at Ryan as she nudged Marisa.

"So, I'm headed to get a bite to eat at this little cozy restaurant in Camden Town."

"Camden Town?" Marisa asked.

"Yes. It's an inner city district just northwest of London. You could find several markets, usually flooded with tourist and local residents."

Marisa looked at Tiffany who was now staring at Ryan.

"The restaurant is called *Jamon Jamon*. They have great cocktails and the food is really good. Would you like to join me?" He asked as he smiled at Tiffany.

"We-ell—" Marisa started out with a doubtful tone.

"Absolutely. We'd love to," Tiffany interrupted as she heard the doubt in Marisa's voice.

"Great. Let me go grab my car."

Ryan darted off to the back of the building, and disappeared around the corner.

Tiffany slowly turned towards Marisa, suddenly feeling a pinch on her arm. "Ouch!" she said, grabbing the side of her arm.

"Are you serious, Tiffany? We've been out all day. I'm tired, my feet hurt, my back aches—and I'm hungry!" Marisa paused as she thought about that. "I hope their food is good!"

Tiffany laughed as she hugged her.

Soon a white, four-door, convertible Maserati pulled up to where Marisa and Tiffany stood. Ryan got out and opened both doors.

"Ladies, your chariot awaits."

"And what a chariot it is," Tiffany said as he waved his hand towards the door.

Tiffany looked at Marisa. "I call dibs on the front seat!" she said as she walked towards the car.

"But of course you would," was her sardonic reply as she climbed into the back seat.

Ryan closed the doors. "Buckle up, ladies," he said as they headed to Camden Town.

Marisa watched as the buildings faded and the grass began to, once again, line the highway. She had been engaged in a nice conversation with Ryan and Tiffany, but her thoughts started to drift. Their voices faded softly in the distance and her thoughts became louder and louder.

She thought of the new apartment and the new life she was about to make for herself in London. She thought of a life away from all the echoes of her past. She would no longer have to pretend to ignore the passivity of her mother. She felt relief in the thought of not having to put on niceties with her father, knowing what she knew and what she suspected about the woman in California. She could immerse herself there in London, in her work and in her new home.

Suddenly, Marisa placed her hands over her face. Her eyes tightened shut as the memories of the rape flooded her mind. Like a thief, it clawed away at her thoughts of happiness. And she felt as if she were swaying back and forth.

A few moments later, Tiffany noticed that Marisa had disengaged from the conversation. "Hey back there. Marisa? Where are you, girl?"

Ryan glanced in the rearview mirror.

Her hands still covered her face as the memories of that night grew larger and larger in her mind.

"Is everything okay, little lady?"

Marisa raised her head from her hands. "What did you say?"

"I asked if everything was okay?"

"No!" Marisa said angrily. "What did you say?"

Ryan looked at Tiffany.

"What did you just call me?" She had become visibly agitated.

"Mari, what's wrong with you?" Tiffany said, confused with her friend's attitude. "He only asked if everything was okay." She couldn't hide her embarrassment, and turned to apologize for Marisa's behavior.

"That's okay," Ryan said empathetically. "I know you guys are tired. It's been a long day. My sister eats me alive when she's had a long hard day," he said in an effort to ease the awkward moment.

"I apologize, Ryan. I'm just really tired. Would you guys mind just dropping me off at the hotel?"

"Sure thing. I understand," he replied.

The car soon pulled up to the hotel where Marisa and Tiffany were staying. Everyone had been quiet during the rest of the ride.

"My apologies again, Ryan."

"No problem. It was a pleasure meeting you," he said.

Marisa smiled as he opened the door for her, thoughtfully she headed down the walkway toward the entrance of the hotel.

Tiffany sighed as Ryan sat back in the car. Looking at him, she said, "I'm sorry. I think I need to go and make sure my girl is okay. She's had a really rough go of things these past few weeks."

"Ah, don't worry about it. I understand. Maybe we can get together another time."

Tiffany smiled as she reached for the door handle.

"No, no," he said as he got out of the car and walked around to open the door for her.

"Thank you, Ryan. You're such a great guy."

"Thanks, my father taught me a few things. One was that a lady should never have to open her own door when a man is present."

"Well, your father is to be commended." Tiffany started towards the hotel when...

"I'd really like to see you again," Ryan yelled out to her. When she turned around, he was now standing inside the driver's side door, about to get in.

"I'd like that," Tiffany said, smiling sheepishly. "Goodnight, Ryan."

"Goodnight," he replied as he watched her disappear inside the hotel.

Tiffany walked into the room. The bathroom door was closed but she could hear the sound of the shower running. She sat on the side of the bed for a moment. The lights from the airport slightly lit the now darkened room. The only other light present was the light that gently showed from under the bathroom door.

She got up and sat in a chair that was snugly placed in the corner of the room near the window. Her hand reached up for the handle to close the curtains. Her eyes began to fill with tears as the noise that came from the shower continued. Tiffany sat there wondering about the pain Marisa must be going through and how helpless she felt in comforting her.

The water from the shower stopped and a few quiet moments passed before Marisa emerged from the bathroom with a white towel wrapped around her body and one around her head. Reaching for the lamp switch on the nightstand she noticed the silhouette of Tiffany's body from the light that filtered out from the bathroom. She wrapped the towel a bit closer around herself as she sat on the edge of the bed. She took a deep breath.

"I'm so sorry, Tiffany. I don't know what came over me." She stood up and started pacing. "I was thinking, just *thinking*, when all of a sudden these other thoughts just flooded my mind. I tried to fight them."

Tiffany sat silently and listened as she continued.

"Then I thought, I thought I heard Ryan say…"

"Heard him say what, Marisa?" she said, leaning forward in the chair.

"I thought I heard him say 'little lady'."

"No, Marisa, he never said that and if he did, so what? What significance does that have?"

Marisa paused for a second. "Matt," she blurted out.

"Matt? What does Matt have to do with any of this—?" Tiffany stopped mid-sentence as she slowly raised up from the chair. "Oh my God! Is Matt the one who…?"

"I don't know!" She placed her hands over her face as she began to cry. "I don't know!"

"What do you mean you don't know? What makes you think it was him then?"

Marisa sat on the side of the bed. "I don't know if it was him, Tiffany."

"Then why?" she paused. "Is he the one who refers to you as 'little lady'?"

She looked up and said, "Yes." Tiffany sat down on the bed beside her as Marisa tried to recall the events of that night leading up to the rape. "I was headed to the dorm to change for the party. I thought I heard a sound but I didn't see anything or anyone."

Tiffany laid her hand on top of hers. "Rissa, why did you walk home alone?"

"I wasn't thinking," she said. "I was angry because of my dad not staying till the end of graduation. I don't even know if he saw me walk across the stage for my degree. I was angry. Then my mom was trying to cover for him, and knowing about the woman in California…I don't know, I was just a mess!"

"So, where does Matt fit in all this?"

"Well," Marisa turned towards her. "When I finally got to the dorm, I was searching for my key when he stepped out of the shadows."

"What? Was he following you?" Tiffany was becoming visibly angry.

"I don't know if he was following me or not. All I remember was that he was there. He made small talk and referred to me as "little lady".

Tiffany stood up and began pacing the floor, shaking her head in disbelief. "He never struck me as that kind of person, different maybe…but rape?" she ranted.

Softly, Marisa murmured, "He's here."

Tiffany stopped pacing. "He who? Who's here?" She was now glaring at Marisa.

"Matt."

"What the hell is he doing here?" she said angrily.

"I'm not really sure. Every time I see him I freak out and run."

"Well, when did you see him last?"

"On my way here as I waited for my connecting flight. I was sitting there when I felt this presence behind me. Then I heard this voice that said 'well, hello, little lady'."

Tiffany starting pacing again. "Geez Rissa."

"When I looked up and saw it was him, I guess I panicked. I don't even remember if I said anything. I just ran to the gate. I could barely find my ticket," she said and began sobbing again.

Tiffany hugged her in an effort to console her best friend. "I'm so sorry, Rissa. I'm so sorry."

Gently she rocked her back and forth. They both sat there in the darkness for a while. Marisa was terrified at the thought of Matt being in London. Then Tiffany broke the silence.

"Maybe you ought to get a gun."

"No! Girl, I'm scared to death of guns. I don't think I could ever take another person's life."

Tiffany thought for a moment. "Well, maybe a taser."

"Maybe I could get one of those, I guess."

"You need something. I know we don't really know Ryan like that but I get a good vibe from him, Marisa, and you know I'm not usually wrong. Maybe he can check on you from time to time."

"I don't know, Tiffany. He's a stranger."

Tiffany's frustration increased. "Well, I'm not asking you to go out with the guy. Just let him, maybe, call you or something from time to time."

"I don't know," Marisa said with reluctance in her voice. "I'll think about it. I'm going to bed."

"Yeah, I guess we'd better," Tiffany said in agreement. "Besides, we have some more apartments to look at tomorrow. I have a feeling we're going to find the ideal one for you."

"I hope so. I'm exhausted and I only have a couple of weeks before I start this new job."

The next morning Glenna stopped in to pick up Marisa and Tiffany. "Good morning, ladies. I hope you both slept well."

"I slept great," Tiffany responded, and touched her friend's shoulder. "How about you?"

Marisa smiled. "Oh, I'm still a bit exhausted from yesterday but I slept okay."

"Not very convincing, is she, Glenna?" Tiffany said from the back seat.

"Having that mother's intuition, I get the feeling she's covering something," Glenna said. "My daughter would get that way often after her freshman year at college."

"She did?" Marisa asked inquisitively.

"Yes," Glenna responded. "She had a very difficult first year. She became very withdrawn at one point."

Marisa sat quietly, gazing at the older woman.

"I thought it was because she didn't really know anyone and she had never been that far from home."

"Where did she attend, Glenna?" Marisa couldn't help but wonder if the women's daughter could have been a victim of rape. Much of what the woman was saying sounded like what she had been experiencing.

"She attended Paris American Academy."

"Oh, isn't that a school for fashion?" Tiffany chimed in from the back seat.

"Why yes, it is. You know much about it?"

"Well, only that someone I know from college spoke of going there after she graduated."

"Oh, I see."

Glenna looked over at Marisa who was sitting quietly. "You okay, dear?" her voice sounding concerned.

"So, did your daughter go back after her first semester? Did she say why she didn't like it, or—or did anything happen?" Marisa inquired, directing the conversation back to Glenna's daughter.

"Well, we have spoken of it on occasion, but—oh!—here we are, ladies. Chateau'La Maison."

The girls turned to see a beautiful building with red brick covering the face. Flower pots hung from the window sills that scaled two stories high. They were filled with an array of pink, yellow and purple blooming flowers that brought a feeling of spring.

Three steps with black wrought-iron rails led up to a rustic hobbit-style door. A potted plant hung from a nail that had been driven into the brick wall and on either side of the steps were flower beds of chrysanthemums. Marisa felt a calming peace envelop her body.

"This is it," she said softly as her eyes scaled the walls. Glenna had gotten out of the car to unlock the door. "Tiffany," Marisa said as she slowly got out of the car, "this is it."

"Girl, you haven't even seen the inside yet."

"I know, but this is it. I just know it."

"Come on, ladies. Let's take a look inside."

Tiffany and Glenna went inside as Marisa slowly walked up the three stairs that led to the beautifully painted door. She touched some of the flowers and the lush green ivory that lined the walls. The entrance gave way to a small table that sat flush against the soft pale green wall.

Right above it was a victorian-styled, oval-shaped mirror. To the left was a door that led into a small room that could be used for office space. Further down the hallway was an opening large enough for living space. And a small brick fireplace was nestled in the corner.

"So what do you think?" Glenna said as she turned towards Marisa.

"I love it. It's just like I have imagined. The bedrooms are so beautiful." Marisa ran her fingers across the painted wall. "The soft green is so calming. I can't wait to decorate it."

Tiffany hurried towards the kitchen.

"Oh, and look at this kitchen, Tiffany!" Marisa said excitedly as she turned around in the middle of the floor.

"Wait a minute, girly," she cautioned her. "Let's not get too excited. You don't know if you can afford this."

Marisa turned towards Glenna. A look of concern now covering her face.

Glenna smiled. "Your budget is fifteen hundred, and the owners are long-time clients of mine. They want someone here that will love it and enjoy it as much as they did when they lived here. They are willing to rent it out for twelve hundred."

Marisa gasped as she looked at Tiffany. They slowly began moving toward each other as smiles spread across each of their faces. The girls reached out their hands and wiggled their fingers. Suddenly they screamed as they hugged each other.

"Twelve hundred!" Marisa said as they jumped up and down in the middle of the kitchen.

"Well, I see you ladies are quite pleased," Glenna said as she smiled at their excitement.

Out of breath, Marisa turned to her. "Where do I sign?"

"Let's head back to the office and draw up the papers."

Marisa turned in the middle of the room. "Oh my god, I don't want to leave!" They headed out the door and back to the office. "I'll see you soon, my new home," she said as the car headed down the cobblestone street.

"Me, too!" Tiffany echoed.

Marisa turned to look at her. For a moment neither one of them said a word. Then a burst of laughter filled the car.

They arrived back at the Glenna's office a little while later. "Have a seat," she said, motioning for Marisa to sit in the chair in front of her desk.

"Thank you." Noticing that Tiffany wasn't there, she looked back towards the door, and spotted Tiffany standing in the doorway of Ryan's office.

"Hello, stranger." She tapped lightly on Ryan's door.

"Well, hello there, Tiffany," he stopped looking at the papers that covered his desk. "How's the apartment hunting going?"

"Well, actually Marisa did find a place in Camden Town."

"Oh, really?" Ryan said with excitement. "That's great!"

"Yeah, it's this cute little place that has such a cozy cottage feel."

"Oh, wow," he responded.

"Yes," Tiffany paused as she sought for words. "Well, um…" He stared at Tiffany with anticipation. "I wanted to apologize again for last night. I felt quite bummed about the way it ended."

"Aw, that's okay. Really, I understand." Ryan tapped his hands on his desk. "So, maybe you girls can make it up to me."

"Make it up to you?" Tiffany smiled.

"Yes. Today is Friday; it's still early. Maybe we can go to Camden Town and get a bite to eat later."

"Oh, that sounds great but—" she hesitated, "let me check with Marisa first and I will get back with you."

"Sure," Ryan responded. "That's fair."

"Okay," she said as she began backing out of his office. "Talk soon."

Tiffany sat down in the seat next to Marisa.

"I see you couldn't wait to get over to your piece of meat."

Tiffany shoved her shoulder. "He's not a piece of meat. He's a really nice guy."

"Mmm-hhmm…sure," she said teasingly.

"So, what's going on? Have you signed the papers?"

Marisa was visibly excited. "Yes. Glenna went down the hall to make copies. Wait, tomorrow's Saturday!"

"I know," she said with a sigh.

"You're flying out on Sunday and we haven't really did anything but look at apartments."

Tiffany thought this was a great time to share Ryan's proposition. "Well, Ryan asked if, well, since things kinda went down the way they did the other night that maybe we all can hang out." She sat nervously. She wasn't sure how Marisa would respond.

"Oh, wow! That sounds great!" she responded with excitement.

Tiffany was shocked. "What? Really?"

Marisa saw the elation in her eyes. "Girl, I didn't realize your nose was open."

Tiffany leaned back in her chair. "What do you mean?"

Marisa pressed her lips together. "I've seen the way you look at Ryan when he's around."

She tried to play coy. "What are you talking about? I mean, he's a good guy and all but…"

They sat there staring at each other for a moment. Being best friends Tiffany knew she wasn't fooling Marisa. Suddenly they burst into laughter. "Girl, I have a new apartment. I start my new job on Monday. Nothing can dampen my day today."

"Well, alright!" Tiffany high-fived her. "Let's do this! I'll tell Ryan."

Soon Glenna walked back into the office. "Well, ladies, you're all set. You can take possession of the apartment tomorrow."

"Tomorrow?" Marisa exclaimed. She had not anticipated things happening so quickly.

"Yes, tomorrow," the woman said, smiling.

Marisa looked at Tiffany. "It's really happening. London is going to be my home." She placed her right hand on her chest. "My heart is like beating so fast right now."

Glenna tapped on her desk. "Annnddd—" She rattled a set of keys that she held between her fingers. Marisa slowly reached for them as Glenna gently placed them in her hands.

"A new beginning," Marisa said softly as she looked up at Tiffany.

"Yeah, Rissa," she said knowing what she had recently gone through. "A new beginning. You deserve it. Let's tell Ryan!"

Before they could stand up they found him standing in the doorway. "I heard screaming and laughter over here. Does that mean we're on for tonight?" He folded his arms and leaned against the door.

"Abso-friggin-lutely! Let's go!" Marisa said as she rose from the chair.

Ryan looked at Tiffany as she shrugged her shoulders at him. "Okay, well let's go," she said, raising up from the chair.

"Great! I will pull the car around front while you ladies finish up here." Ryan hurried down the hallway and out the building.

Glenna opened her desk drawer. "So, Marisa, you're new to our great city. Here are some bus schedules and a pre-filled bus card."

Marisa took the card along with her rental packet. "Thank you, Glenna."

"You're welcome. You can purchase additional tokens at the bus depots."

"You've been so amazing throughout this whole process. I don't know what I would have done without you."

"Thank you, beautiful," Glenna said as she hugged her. "You have become like a daughter to me in such a short time. Keep in touch. I will be more than happy to be a guide from time to time."

"Yes, that would be great. I may take you up on that, seeing that Tiffany will be flying back to the states on Sunday."

"Oh, will you be coming back?" She turned towards Tiffany who was anxiously eyeing the end of the hallway, no doubt looking for Ryan.

"Tiffany!" Marisa said as she nudged her.

Startled, she turned around. "What?"

"Glenna asked you a question."

"Oh, uh-huh." She mumbled, looking back down the hall.

"Tiffany!"

"I'm sorry. What was the question again?"

"Glenna asked if you were coming back to London.

Tiffany looked her way. "Oh yes, yes," she said, a bit embarrassed when she realized they knew the reason for her being distracted.

"No worries," Glenna said as she chuckled. "I understand you're headed back to the states soon."

"Oh, yes ma'am."

"Will you be coming back soon?"

She smiled at Marisa. "Well, that's the plan. Ms. Webb here can't do without me for too long."

Marisa pinched her friend's shoulder.

"Ouch!"

Suddenly Ryan was standing back at the doorway.

"Are you ready, ladies? Your chariot awaits."

"Sure," Tiffany said, rubbing her arm.

"Are you okay?" He said as they walked down the hall.

"Ohhh, just a bit of a love-hate relationship going on."

"Huh?"

"It's complicated," she chuckled as they walked out the door.

Darkness had begun to slowly cover the evening sky when they arrived in Camden. Things were off to a good start and Marisa was excited that things had begun to fall into place. The music inside Ryan's car seemed to flood Marisa's mind as she closed her eyes and popped her fingers in the air.

Upon hearing Marisa's fingers popping behind her, Tiffany turned around. "Girl, you *are* in a good mood. Now, this is the Marisa I know and love." She smiled, watching Marisa lose herself in the music.

"Yes. Things are looking up," she responded. "I'm ready to just let my hair down and get my party on." Marisa leaned up between the front seats. The street lights sped by while the headlights from the oncoming cars spun a vortex of swirling colors.

"I'm going to stop by my place and pick up my sister...if it's okay with you two."

"Sure thing!" Tiffany said, excited that she was going to meet Ryan's sister.

"Sure, that's cool," Marisa agreed from the back of the car. "At least I won't feel like a third wheel while I'm out with the two of *you*."

"Why Marisa?" Tiffany playfully gasped. Placing her hand on her chest as she shook her head. "Surely you jest."

Marisa pushed her on the side of her head with her finger. "No, I surely *don't* jest."

They laughed as Ryan pulled up to a white and silver building that looked like something from the future. The floors were built to look almost like waves. Straight towards the back you could see a rounded black marble counter with silver trim.

Two people could be seen assisting guests who were standing at the counter. At the entrance stood a middle-aged salt and pepper haired doorman dressed in a white shirt with a black tuxedo and red tie.

"I'll be right back, ladies, unless you would like to come up."

"Sure!" Tiffany said in amazement. She couldn't take her eyes off of the incredible-looking building.

"Great!" Ryan responded as he ran around and opened the door for them, then handed the valet his keys to park the car.

Tiffany looked at Marisa. "Well."

"Well, indeed," she said as they watched the valet drive off in the car.

"This way, ladies," Ryan said motioning towards the door.

Marisa and Tiffany followed him towards the entrance of the lobby. The doorman greeted Ryan by his last name and opened the door for them to all walk through.

Ryan stopped by the concierge desk. "Any mail for me, Vivian?" he asked the woman behind the counter.

"No, Mr. Mason. Oh, there was a phone call from your mother," the woman added.

"Thank you, Vivian, I'll be sure to return *that* call," he smiled and tapped on the counter.

"You'd better," the woman replied, smiling.

Walking over to a wooden-frame door, he pushed the button for the twelfth floor. In a matter of seconds the door of the elevator began to open.

"Um...is this a rocket ship or an elevator?" Tiffany said jokingly.

Ryan laughed. "It is pretty fast, isn't it?"

"You think? she said as they stepped on the elevator.

Almost seconds later, they exited the elevator and walked a few doors down to the end of the hallway. Ryan unlocked the door, and a voice echoed from the kitchen.

"Is that my handsome big brother?"

"But of course. Unless you were expecting someone else."

"No, you lug," the young woman said as she hugged him.

"I have some people I want you to meet," he said.

Tiffany and Marisa stepped in from the hallway.

"Oh, okay."

"Tiffany…Marisa, this is Indra, my one and only little sister. My heart."

"Aw, Ryan, you're so sweet," Indra said, blushing. Remembering her manners, "Hello, Marisa…Tiffany," she said, reaching out her hand. "I'm so pleased to meet you. So, you're Tiffany, eh?" she said while shaking Tiffany's hand.

"Um…yes, I am," Tiffany said, and turned to look at Marisa with a worried look on her face.

"Oh, no worries," Indra said. "It's just that my brother came home the other night saying how he had met this beautiful young lady. He went on and on…"

Tiffany became a bit embarrassed as she turned towards Ryan who was looking at her with a bit of embarrassment himself.

"So, let me show you two around while my little big mouth sister goes and gets dressed," lovingly pushing Indra's head.

"Oh yeah, that's right. We're going out. I'll be ready in a flash." Indra disappeared into a bedroom to the left of the living room.

"So, ladies, we are now standing in the middle of the living room." Ryan continued walking around the condo. "Over here is the fireplace and straight behind you there is the kitchen and down that short hallway is my room. It's a mess right now."

This made the girls laugh.

"If you walk over here…" he said, gesturing in a different direction. Marisa and Tiffany followed him to a half wall. On the other side was another seating area. The windows went from one side of the glassed balcony to the other. In the middle were sliding doors that led to an outside balcony that overlooked the city.

Tiffany was enamored by the view. "This is breathtaking," she said holding onto the balcony and looking at the city lights that surrounded her like stars in the sky.

"This is such a beautiful view, Ryan," Marisa said, also looking out over the balcony.

"Thank you. I'm glad you both like it." He walked over to where Tiffany stood. She smiled sheepishly as she looked up at him.

"I'm ready!" Indra called out.

Ryan turned towards the door. "Um...well, let's get this show on the road. We're off to see the wizardry of London."

They all laughed as they headed out.

"So, where are we going?" Indra asked him.

"Well, I'm surrounded by several beautiful ladies who want to have a good time, so we're going to the Button Down Disco."

"Like whoa!" she said excitedly. "That's like one of the hottest clubs in London. We should have a great time there."

"Sounds like our kind of place," Tiffany said with the same enthusiasm.

Arriving at the club, Ryan let the girls out at the door and went to park the car.

"Wow! This is nice," Tiffany said as she looked around.

People were entering and exiting the building when they walked up. You could hear the music bellowing out the door whenever it was opened. Tiffany began popping her fingers and swaying with the music. Ryan ran from across the street.

"Here we are. Let's go on inside."

The club was crowded. Balloons were everywhere, floating mostly near the ceiling. Others were being held by some of the club goers. A bar sat directly adjacent to the DJ's booth, but the main seating was strategically placed around the dance floor. People stood around laughing, chatting, or dancing to the music. Ryan was known by the owner and was able to get VIP seats for them all.

"Okay, Mr. Golden Child. You got it like that?" Tiffany said as she smiled.

"Nah, just an old college buddy."

"Mmm-hmm, okay." She winked at the girls.

"Hey, you ladies want something to drink? I'm going to head over to the bar."

"I'll have an Apple Martini," Tiffany said as she picked up her purse."

"Tiffany, please put your purse down." Indra gently nudged her purse back towards the seat. "Ryan will never allow you to pay."

"What about you Indra? Marisa?"

"I'll have a *Mercury*."

"What's a Mercury?" Marisa asked inquisitively.

"Well," she began to explain. "It's, um, greengage sorbet, gin, lemon juice and Prosecco. It's really yummy."

Marisa thought for a second. "Okay, I'll have one too," she said, and looked up at Ryan.

"Okay, I'll be right back."

"So, Indra, I understand you're in college. What are you majoring in?"

"I'm actually getting a degree in psychology. This is my third year."

"Oh, I was under the impression that you were just starting."

Indra chuckled. "No, I went to a different school my first two years, and transferred to UCL."

"UCL?" Marisa asked.

"Yes, University College of London."

"Sounds like you're moving right along."

"Yes, my brother is such an inspiration for me. You know, he's come through some rough times having to help our mum and myself. He's making his mark in the real estate business."

"Yeah, it's obvious," Marisa said making reference to all she'd seen and heard about the man.

"What about you, Marisa?" Indra turned the conversation around.

"Well, I graduated in Marketing. I'm actually here to start a new job with a company here in London."

"Oh wow! That's great," she exclaimed. "What about you, Tiffany?"

Tiffany's back was turned as she watched Ryan in the distance. Marisa nudged her.

"Have a hard time focusing lately, do you?" she said, referring to the realty office event.

"Oh, what?" Tiffany said as she turned around in her seat.

Indra smiled. "My brother really likes you, you know."

Tiffany blushed. "Really?"

"Really." She looked over where her brother was standing. "He's spoken of you everyday from the day he met you, and that's saying a lot when it comes to Ryan."

"Why do you say that?" Marisa asked.

"Well, other than helping me and my mum which is enough in and of itself, he was engaged."

"Engaged?" Tiffany was all ears as she leaned forward in her seat.

"Yes," Indra said, a look of sadness coming across her face. "He's not engaged anymore, though."

Tiffany quietly expelled a sigh of relief. "What happened? Why isn't he engaged anymore?"

"Well..." she said hesitantly.

They had not seen Ryan coming back towards the table.

"Here you go, ladies." he said, stepping up to the table. "A Mercury for you," he said as he gave Marisa her drink. "One for you, Indra, and an apple martini for you, Tiffany."

"Thank you." Tiffany took a sip of her drink. "Now, that's a good martini," she said as she toasted the others sitting around her.

"So, what were you ladies talking about?"

"Oh, just stuff. College and my business tycoon of a brother," Indra said as she gently punched him on the shoulder.

He laughed. "Nah. I'm just blessed to have amazing people in my life," he said, hugging his sister. "Tiffany, would you like to dance?" He held out his hand.

"Um, sure thing, kiddo." Tiffany waved at the girls as she and Ryan headed for the dance floor.

"Now, what were you about to say, Indra? I mean, about Ryan's engagement?"

"It's a long story. Maybe I shouldn't say anything. It's a very sensitive subject for him so...I'd rather he said something. If he decides to, that is."

"Oh, I understand," Marisa said as she took of sip from her drink. "Sometimes life takes unexpected turns." She had begun to think about her own secrets. "We think it could never happen to us. But it can. Things that can change your life forever. Sometimes those things can be so tragic that you just bury them deep inside. You suppress them even though you know in your heart it's not the healthiest thing to do."

Indra, having a sense that she was speaking of something in particular, listened closely.

Marisa stared into her glass. "You think you know people, then you find out that all they have said, and the person they've portrayed themselves to be, was a portrait of painted lies—" she stopped, remembering her company. "Oh, I apologize, Indra. Here I am going on and on."

"No, it's okay," she said. "You're absolutely right. Life can be that way sometimes. Even when we try to be smart about it, it outsmarts us." Indra looked out at Ryan and Tiffany on the dance floor. "Thing is, we can't beat ourselves up. We have to keep breathing. Keep living. We have to make the best of what we have in the moment. Know what I mean?" she stated, and looked back at Marisa.

"Yes. You're absolutely right."

"Hey, Marisa!"

Marisa looked up to see Tiffany and Ryan coming towards them from the dance floor. Someone was walking closely behind them. Winded, Tiffany stepped up to the table. "Look! Look who I found on the dance floor!" she said, stepping aside.

"Patrick?" Marisa said in surprise as she leaned forward to get a better look. She watched one of the flood lights move and hit Patrick's face as he stepped closer to the table. "Patrick! Wow! What a surprise!"

"Marisa? You were the last person I expected to see here in Camden."

Marisa smiled. "Yeah."

"Oh, hello. I'm Patrick, a college friend of Marisa's."

"I'm sorry. Patrick this is Indra."

"Hello, Indra. Nice name."

"Thank you. A pleasure." She reached out to shake his hand. "It looks like you've already met Ryan, Indra's brother."

He turned towards Ryan. "Yeah. Tiffany introduced us. This place is crashing, isn't it?" he said as he turned towards the crowded room.

"Yes. It's pretty hyped in here. A very nice place," Marisa said as she looked around.

"Well, it was good seeing you." Patrick looked at Marisa. "Guess I'll head back. I'm with a group of friends. Don't want them to think I've gotten lost." He turned to walk away. "Hope to see you around, Marisa."

"Um, sure. Me too."

He smiled before disappearing into the crowd. A couple of hours passed while they all mingled around the table. All of a sudden Marisa heard a growling sound.

"What was that?" Ryan said, looking around.

Looking over at Tiffany, Marisa burst into laughter.

"What? What did I miss?" he looked around again.

Marisa was laughing hysterically, and pointing at Tiffany.

"It was my stomach," she said embarrassingly. "I'm hungry."

Everyone at the table began to laugh.

"Hmm, there is an awesome place just a few blocks away. We can head over there."

Still laughing, they all agreed and headed out that way.

4

Forsaking The Memories

The next morning the hotel room was still. The only sounds that could be heard was the air conditioner and the intermittent snoring that came from Marisa as she slept. The sun rays became brighter through the cracks of the barely closed hotel curtains.

Awakened by the snoring, Tiffany opened one eye. Her face pressed against the pillow, she raised her head and turned towards Marisa who was still in a deep sleep. She listened for a minute waiting for the next snore to sound.

When nothing came, she slowly laid her head back on the pillow, sighing a breath of relief, but that relief would not last long. Marisa snored again. This time Tiffany grabbed her pillow and hit Marisa.

Startled, she sat straight up. "Huh, what?"

"Girl! What did you drink last night?" Tiffany said a bit annoyed from being rudely awakened. "I don't ever remember hearing you snore."

Marisa slowly laid back on her pillow. "Oh, my head," she moaned as she placed her hand on her temples.

"I didn't hit you that hard."

She continued rubbing her temples. "I think it was those drinks. You know I'm not an alcoholic like you." Closing her eyes, Marisa laid her arm over her head.

"I'm going to need you to not ever drink again. Hold on...you were sleeping really hard, let me check this bed." Tiffany pulled the covers up and felt the mattress near Marisa. "Did you pee your pj's, you drunk?"

Marisa slowly opened her eyes to look at her. "Could you stop talking, please?"

"No! I thought I felt something wet and warm during the night."

Marisa turned over. "Are you serious, Tiffany? You know I didn't wet the bed."

"Girl, I'm just saying. You were doing some hard snoring," she said, mimicking her snoring.

Marisa punched her in the arm then fell backwards onto her pillow. "Ow! My head!"

Tiffany laughed. "You know they have people that can help you with that anger, right?" Laying back, she rubbed her arm. They lay there, silently, for a while until the alarm on Marisa's phone went off.

"It's nine o'clock already?" she mumbled disappointedly.

Tiffany, her face now buried in the pillow, sighed. "Your alarm is wrong."

"No, it's not. We've got to get up."

"Noooo! I'm too tired," she whined as she turned her head away.

"Last night was really nice, wasn't it?" Marisa said as she stared up at the rotating ceiling fan.

"Uh-huh," Tiffany responded.

"I definitely didn't expect to see Patrick there, did you?"

Tiffany turned over on her back. "No, I didn't. Out of all the places in London…"

"Yeah," Marisa said wistfully.

"He looked pretty good in his little tight jeans."

"Yeah, I saw you looking at his, um, tight jeans." Marisa hit her with a pillow.

"I was not!"

Marisa chuckled. "Mmm-hmm."

Tiffany looked over at her. She had pulled the covers back and was sitting on the side of the bed. "He is fine and all. Not as fine as Ryan, but he's fine. So, you think he's going to be here long?"

"Who?" Marisa said as she slowly raised from the bed.

"Patrick. Who else am I talking about?"

"I don't know. He did say that he would be coming to London after graduation." Marisa started walking towards the bathroom. Reaching the door she turned around. "I wonder if they hooked up that night."

"They who?" Tiffany was now sitting up.

"That girl and Patrick…"

"Your guess is as good as mine. I don't remember seeing him at the party very long. I think he left?"

Marisa felt a chill come over her. She began to wonder if Patrick had come to the dorm that night. "He left? By himself?"

"I think so, but I can't be sure." Tiffany looked over at her. "Why...you'd be jealous?" she chuckled.

"Of course not," Marisa said trying to smile while the curious thoughts ran through her mind.

"Oh, wait! Yeah, I do remember seeing him talking to her. He *could* have left with her."

"Oh, he did?" Marisa felt a sense of relief.

"Oh, girl stop! I know you liked Patrick. Why didn't you ever tell him?"

"I didn't—because he was such a jerk with all his little groupies," she said as she curled the ends of her hair with a curling iron. "Every time I saw him he always seemed to be flirting with one girl or another."

"Marisa, he was a football player, you know how that goes. Girls flock all over those guys."

"And I wasn't going to be one of them. Well, I've got things to do since I now have an apartment to decorate. Get up, Tiffany!"

"Unngghh! I'm tired," she moaned as she buried her head once again in her pillow. She felt the pillow Marisa had thrown earlier slowly being moved from off the middle of her back. "Ah-ah!" Tiffany said as she raised her hand and wiggled her finger in the air.

"What?" Marisa said with an innocent look on her face.

"I told you, they have people that can help you with your anger issues," she said, raising her head from the pillow. Throwing the pillow anyway, Marisa headed back to the bathroom.

"Come on, Tiff...get up! We have a lot to do today."

Suddenly Marisa felt the vibration from a big thump in the room. She peeped out the bathroom door just in time to see one of Tiffany's hands raising from the other side of the bed. Slowly, her head appeared.

"What happened? Are you okay?" she said through a mouth full of toothpaste.

Resting on her knees, Tiffany laid her head on the bed. "I turned over and the next thing I knew I was on the floor."

"You need help?" she asked with a slight smirk.

"Nah. I'm good." Tiffany slowly lifted herself back onto the edge of the bed.

"Good, now I can really laugh," she said as she disappeared back into the bathroom. "So, I saw this store when we were in the market yesterday. It had the cutest vintage furniture. I was thinking about going by there today. There was this beautifully distressed white hall table that would fit really nicely near the door."

"Oh, really?" Tiffany's voice was muzzled. "Do you remember the name of the store?"

"No, but I remember how to get there, that is once we get to the market area. They had a few nice pieces but I'm not going to decorate all vintage. I think I want a few modern pieces, too. Oh! I came across this really nice wall piece...a vintage bicycle. It was kinda rusted like. The wheels had like these old fashioned spindles. It was blackish-gray in color, but I thought I'd spray paint it yellow or something bright. What do you think?"

No answer came from the bedroom. Marisa listened. "So, what do you think, Tiff?" Still there was no answer. "Tiffany! Tiffany?"

Marisa walked out of the bathroom as she brushed her hair from one side to the other. Tiffany had lain back on the bed. Her arms were sprawled out on either side. She walked over and noticed that she had fallen back to sleep. Smiling and shaking her head, she quietly finished dressing and headed out the door.

Marisa hailed a cab a few minutes later. "Camden Markets, please," she said as she got into the back seat of the white cab.

In the quiet of the car, thoughts of seeing Patrick last night crossed her mind. She knew he would be coming but never expected to actually see him. She wondered if his being there with someone else was the reason for his abrupt departure.

"Stop!" Marisa whispered to herself as she quieted the thoughts racing through her mind. She took a deep breath. *Okay, where was that store?* she thought looking outside the window. The area had started looking more familiar to her now.

"Here we are, madam. Camden Markets," the driver said. "Any particular place?"

"No, you can put me out at the next corner." Moments later, the cab came to a stop. "Thank you," she said as she paid the driver.

Standing on the sidewalk, Marisa looked around. The street was filled with people going about their day. The aroma of various cuisines filled the air. It was early, but the city was already wide awake.

People sat outside under restaurant awnings as waiters and waitresses scurried about taking orders, or serving tables. Marisa noticed the sign she had seen the day before. *Okay, that store should be...oh, wait!* She thought to herself as she pulled out her cell phone. She remembered that she had recorded the name of the store. "Planet Bazaar" the recording stated. *Yes, that's it.*

About a half block away, Marisa noticed a familiar building. *I think that's it.* She picked up her pace as she began walking in that direction. Soon she was standing in the front of a brick building with grey doors. The windows of the store had a slight blue-gray tint to them. She pressed her face against the window to get a better look inside.

Yep, this is it. Opening the door, the smell of new furniture filled the air.

"Hello. Thank you for stopping in."

Marisa turned to see a five-foot eight, reddish-haired woman coming towards her. Her hand out-stretched to welcome her. "My name is Mecca." She shook Marisa's hand.

"Hello," she said, shaking hers.

"So, is there anything in particular that you're looking for?"

"Actually," Marisa began looking around, "I was in here yesterday and saw a beautiful vintage—" Just as she was talking about it, she spotted the table she was about to describe. "That's it. That's what I'm looking for right there." She pointed to an off-white distressed painted wall table. Mecca followed behind as Marisa walked toward it.

"Oh, this is one of the rare pieces we recently got in. It's a vintage piece from a popular Soho farmhouse."

Marisa ran her fingers across the top of the furniture. "It's beautiful," she replied. "What's the cost?"

"Two hundred ninety-nine pounds," Mecca responded. "That would be, um, three hundred seventy dollars and forty-nine cents in American money."

Marisa pulled out the drawers to take a look at the interior of the table. "I think this will work just fine," she said smiling. "I'll take it."

"Awesome. Let me go get a tag to mark the piece sold. Let me know if you spot anything else you may like."

Mecca walked away. Marisa was excited. She had bought her first piece of furniture. In the middle of her furniture hunting, her phone rang. It was Tiffany.

"Where are you?"

"I didn't want to wake you. I knew you were tired. I came down to Camden to that furniture store I told you about."

"Oh, you're just going to go shopping without me, huh? Miss 'I Need Your Help, Tiffany'."

"Stop, sleepy head," Marisa said laughing. "Remember the lecture you always give *me* on how long you've been knowing me?"

"Yes, what's your point?"

"I know *you*, Tiff. When you're tired, you're tired. You don't like to be woken up. So, I just let you sleep."

"Humph, you're right about that," she murmured. "Well, since you left me, I'm going to go hang out with Ryan...seeing that I'm leaving soon and all."

"Oh, Tiffany, that's right. I wasn't thinking. I'm so sorry. I should have woken you up—"

Tiffany cut her off. "Oh, ah-ah, girl! Don't be singing the blues to me now," she said playfully.

"Come on, Tiff, I'm sorry."

"No, honey your goose is cooked. Roasted. Done! See you later tonight."

"Tiffany!"

"Bye," she said. "Hanging up the phone now."

Marisa wasn't sure if she was just joking around. "Are you really upset?"

She sighed. "Really, Marisa? How long have we been knowing each other?"

Marisa dropped her head. "Oh, gosh, Tiffany, please not that." She could hear her laughing on the other end.

"But I'm sure glad I'm getting the opportunity to hang out with Ryan without you."

Marisa gasped. "Tiff!"

"Girl, you know I'm *kinda* playing."

"I caught that *kinda* part."

"Honey, bye, I've got to hurry and get dressed before Ryan gets here. Enjoy your shopping."

"I will. You enjoy your little outing with Ryan."

"Little?" Tiffany replied. "It's bout to go down, girly. Tootles," she said as she hung up the phone.

Marisa chuckled as she placed her phone back in her purse. She continued to look around the store when she saw an old vintage mirror. She thought it would go well with the other table she had just purchased.

"Wow! Nice vintage mirror."

A male voice echoed from behind her. Marisa turned around to see Patrick standing there.

"Oh, hi! Um...wow! This is weird."

"Weird? How so?" He leaned back on a nearby table and crossed his arms.

"Seeing you here. Like, did you see me come in here or something?"

"Actually, I saw you when you got out of the cab. I was sitting outside a restaurant having some brunch."

"Oh, okay. Alone?" she asked inquisitively.

"Nah. I was with a friend of mine. We were just finishing up and I came over where I saw you disappear."

Marisa found herself trying not to blush. "I saw this beautiful vintage table and since I finally found a place—"

Patrick interrupted her. "You found a place? That's great!" he said, giving her a high-five.

"Yes, it's not very far, just right outside of Camden."

"Oh, sweet. Well, um, we've got to do lunch or dinner or something since you're so close."

"Yeah, sure." She looked up and saw Mecca heading in their direction.

"So, I have the ticket to put on your beautiful wall table," she said, waving the sold ticket in the air.

"Oh, thank you." Marisa turned towards Patrick. "Um, Mecca, this is Patrick. We took some foreign language classes together at a college back home."

"Ah, pleasure to meet you. Are you shopping as well?"

"Oh, no," he said shaking his head. "Just saw Marisa here and came in to say hello."

"Well, let me know if you require any additional assistance. I won't be far away. Again, it was a pleasure, Patrick," she said as she extended her hand once again to shake his.

"No, the pleasure was all mine."

Mecca looked at Marisa. "Charming fellow," she said as she smiled and walked away.

Patrick brushed his hand through his hair as he looked at Marisa.

"Yeah, yeah," she said as she walked off to look at more furniture.

Patrick followed close behind. "So, where did you say your apartment was?"

Marisa didn't respond, she kept on walking.

"Oh, it's like that?"

"What do you mean?" she said turning around.

"You trying to keep where you live your best-kept secret, or something?"

Marisa chuckled. "Who me? Of course not."

"Okay, maybe we can get together later."

"Maybe I can have you over for dinner once I'm settled." She thought this would be a good way of changing the subject.

"That sounds like a winner. Can you cook? You know you modern-day women don't do the kitchen thing."

"I'm not sure what modern-day women you're referring to but, trust me, I know how to cook quite well, sir."

Patrick laughed. "Okay, I guess we will see." He glanced outside the store window. "Well, I gotta go. I fly out tomorrow."

Surprised, Marisa stopped to look at him. "Oh, I thought you were already settled. I mean, like, your friends and all…from last night," she grappled for words.

"Nah, those people were just some acquaintances. I met them through a friend of mine. We just hooked up that night."

"That girl, too?" she asked with curiosity in her voice.

"Ooohhh, do I detect a bit of jealously?"

"Absolutely not!" Marisa looked up in a mirror to get a glimpse of him. "I just didn't think she looked like your type, that's all."

Patrick rested his elbow on his other arm as he rubbed his chin. "Could have fooled me. Sounded just like jealousy," he chuckled.

"It wasn't." Marisa started walking again, acting as if she was more interested in the furniture.

"Well, I'm out. I've got a few things I need to do before it gets late. Take care. Hopefully I'll run into you when I get back and hold you to that dinner."

"Yes. Of course."

Patrick headed towards the door, Marisa turned to watch him leave. Just as he turned to wave, Marisa abruptly turned away, pretending she was looking at a particular piece of furniture. She looked up again as he walked out the door and disappeared from her view.

Quickly grabbing her phone, she called Tiffany. The phone rang several times and went to her voice mail. Marisa hung up and called again. This time Tiffany answered.

"Hey, Tiff. You busy?"

"Um, no, not at all. Just ohh...hanging out with Ryan!" she said sarcastically.

"Guess who I just saw?"

"Who, your psychiatrist? Because obviously you've lost your mind. I'm hanging with Ryan."

"Ha-ha, very funny."

"Okay, who did you see?"

"So, I was in the store when all of a sudden Patrick was standing behind me."

"Patrick? Like how did that happen?"

"He said he was sitting outside at one of the restaurants when he spotted me."

"Oh. Stalker!" Tiffany said playfully.

"He's not a stalker."

Tiffany laughed. "Can we talk about this later? Ryan and I are, well...getting to know each other."

"Eeewww," Marisa remarked.

"Uh, no. Nothing like that, Rissa, geez. Get your mind out of the gutter."

"Hey, I don't know. You know you can be freaky sometimes."

"Wrong," Tiffany said. "Smooches. Talk soon."

Marisa sighed after they hung up. She had expected her friend to be more interested.

"I guess she was distracted with Ryan," Marisa mumbled to herself and shrugged her shoulders.

Mecca, the store associate who was helping her earlier, walked over to see if she had found anything else that she liked. She held up the mirror over the table to see if it was a good match.

"I think I will get this as well."

"Very good choice for the hall table. I will have your total in just a moment."

Marisa continued to pace around the store when she stumbled upon a maple canopy framed bed. The details appeared to be hand carved.

"Oh, this is so adorable." Marisa sat on the bed, then laid down and slowly closed her eyes as a smile came across her face.

"Looks like someone has found her princess bed."

Marisa opened her eyes to see Tiffany and Ryan standing next to the bed. She sat up and stretched her arms as if she had been asleep.

"Girl, quit playing," Tiffany said as she pushed Marisa's arms down.

Marisa fell back on the bed as they all laughed.

"Hello, Ryan. You've been taking care of my BFF?"

Ryan glanced at Tiffany. "I hope so. She's a pretty special lady."

Tiffany looked back at him and then at Marisa. Turning back and forth like a little girl with a frilly dress. She pressed her finger against the deep dimple in her jaw.

"But of course I'm special and guess what…?"

Marisa sat back up on the bed. She looked at Ryan who had a smile on his face, then back at Tiffany.

"Anyywhooo, what have you kids been getting into?"

"It looks like I am definitely coming back to London in about a month."

"What? Stop playing, Tiffany. Are you serious?"

She smiled. "Yep. Ryan took me to this company who's well-known for it's internship program. Get this! They actually designed the building that Ryan lives in."

"Wow!"

"Impressive, if I may say so myself."

Marisa looked at Ryan. "Wait! What about your internship back home?"

"Well, they are giving me the opportunity to do my internship here, and then if I want they will hire me on."

Marisa stood up from the bed. "Get outta here!" The girls screamed, jumping up and down as they hugged each other.

"I'm beginning to think this is like a ritual with you two when exciting news is announced."

Winded, Marisa looked at him, one arm still around Tiffany's neck. "Ryan, you have no idea what this means to me. I thought I was going to be out here alone. Now, my best friend will be here." They suddenly looked at each other, and began hugging all over again.

"I see you ladies are celebrating over here." By this time Mecca joined the crowd.

"I just found out that my best friend," Marisa said motioning towards Tiffany, "will be joining me here in London." She giggled. "She's going back home to the states tomorrow but she'll be back."

"Oh, that's wonderful," Mecca said turning towards Tiffany. "I see congrats are in order. Sounds very exciting for you."

"Yes, it is! I'm so excited," Tiffany said as she looked at Ryan then Marisa. "And to commemorate this moment, I'm going to purchase this bed right here, Mecca."

"Awesome. I guess I had better put a tag on this one for you as well."

Marisa looked at Tiffany and Ryan and smiled.

Later, they all headed back to Ryan's car. Marisa was excited about the direction her life seemed to be going. A new country, a new job and apartment. The nightmares of her past were slowly becoming a thing of the past. Memories she hoped would truly be forgotten.

"Gee, Tiffany, I can't wait for you to get back," she said as Ryan closed the car door.

Tiffany turned towards Marisa who was now strapping on her seat belt. "We're going to have so much fun, and if I may say so myself, we have a really cute guide."

Marisa clasped Ryan's hand. He smiled as he leaned in to kiss Tiffany on the lips.

"Oh, gosh! Will you guys just get a room, will you?"

"Don't tempt us, Rissa," she murmured, at which they all burst out laughing.

"So," Marisa said changing the subject. "Luckily, my furniture will be delivered today. It was a miracle they could get it out so fast," she said clapping her hands excitedly. Suddenly she stopped. Her jubilant attitude was interrupted by a single thought "What time does your plane leave tomorrow?"

Tiffany sighed. "Well, I've got to be at the airport no later than eight o'clock in the morning. My flight leaves at nine."

Marisa pouted. "You sure you can't stay for one more week? Darn, I wish you didn't have to go at all."

"I know. I wish I didn't either. But, don't worry, girlfriend. I will be back before you know it."

"Promise?" Marisa smiled at her.

"Besides, I have a guy who will be anxiously waiting to see me again, at least I hope so anyway." Tiffany poked Ryan in the side.

"Of course I can't wait. But, I'm like Marisa. I wish you didn't have to go at all."

Tiffany felt butterflies in her stomach. "Ryan, that's so sweet."

"Well, its true."

They arrived at the apartment just as the delivery truck was pulling up to the door.

"Look, guys! My furniture is here," Marisa said, clapping her hands. Ryan pulled up to the side of the apartment. Once parked, she jumped out and ran to open the door for the delivery men.

"Hey, guys. Thank you so much for delivering my stuff. I know this isn't your normal delivery time."

"Oh, that's alright. Mecca is a very good friend of mine. I don't mind doing favors for her on occasion," the driver said as he lifted up the back door of his truck. "She doesn't normally do this for people unless she really likes them."

"Oh, wow! Tell Mecca I said thank you from the bottom of my heart."

"Will do, ma'am. So, if you tell us where to place the furniture we can get out of your hair."

The delivery men began pulling furniture off the truck. The first piece was the hall table she had specifically purchased to go under the vintage mirror.

"Okay, this piece goes here in the entrance. You can just sit the mirror down beside it. I'm going to hang it later."

The delivery guys moved the table just beyond the entrance of the doorway. "Would you like for us to mount your mirror? No extra charge...?" The driver picked up a toolbox he had placed on the floor. "Since we're here and we have the tools we might as well."

Marisa thought for a minute. "Okay, that would be great," she said as she showed the man where she wanted the mirror placed. The men situated all the furniture in the apartment. After setting up the bedroom furniture, they finished up the living room.

Marisa stood back admiring the furniture and how it looked in the space. "Isn't this beautiful?" she said, standing there with her arms folded.

"It sure is, Rissa. You made very good choices."

Marisa hugged her. "Thank you, Tiff."

"Um, okay. You're welcome."

"I really mean it. You being here for me, I don't know what I would have done without you."

"What are friends for, girl? I know you would have had my back, too." Tiffany turned towards the bedroom furniture. "I know I'm leaving tomorrow but, um, I'm not sleeping on no couch tonight."

They looked at each other and laughed.

"Hey, the guys are done and getting ready to leave," Ryan said as he walked in from outside.

"Oh, wait!" Marisa ran for her purse. "I want to give them a little something extra for the delivery."

"Whooaaa!" Ryan said, grabbing her arm. "I've already taken care of that."

"Huh?" Marisa said surprisingly.

"They're good."

"Oh, okay." She laid her purse back on the mantle in the kitchen. "You tipped them for me?"

Ryan chuckled. "Yes."

Tiffany laughed. "Are you surprised? Remember, this is a man who won't let you open your own door. Please, bask in the moment."

The girls placed their index fingers and thumbs together, and closed their eyes as they began to chant. Something they often did when they were in college.

"Come on, what are you guys doing?" he asked as he began laughing at them.

Tiffany put her finger over his lips. "Shush! We're basking."

"Yeah, we're basking," Marisa said as she peered at Ryan with one eye opened.

"Okay, yeah." He began to walk backwards. "I'm going to go and let you girls have your, um, *moment.*"

"Uh-huh." Tiffany murmured as she shooed him away.

Later they all stood around in the living room. Ryan had started a fire with the wood that was already stacked on the side of the fireplace. Marisa reached her hands out towards it.

"The fire feels so good. Thank you, Ryan. You're really a nice guy."

Ryan bounded. "You're welcome, Marisa. I have a sister and I would like to think that whomever she decided to date would be a gentleman, too."

"Amen!" Tiffany said out loud as she lifted her hands up in the air.

They all laughed as Ryan gently pushed her arm.

"Well, ladies, I'd better get going. Tiffany, pick you up for the airport tomorrow before I head into work?"

"Sure thing, Ryan." Tiffany got up from sitting in front of the fireplace to walk him to the door.

"See you tomorrow morning."

"You bet, beautiful."

Ryan reached over and gently pecked Tiffany on the lips. She stood at the door as he slowly walked backwards down the steps and then out to his car. Waving goodbye, Tiffany blew him a kiss as he drove away. She slowly walked back into the living room. Marisa sat there staring into the flames.

"Isn't he amazing?" she said as she sat back on the floor.

"Yes, he is," Marisa said a bit somberly.

"What's wrong?" Tiffany nudged her.

"I'm just a bit sad that you're leaving tomorrow."

"Look, I'll be back and Ryan said he'd keep an eye out." She reached in her pocket and pulled out a piece of paper. "Here's his number. He said for you to call him if anything pops off over here."

Marisa took the paper from her. "Thanks, Tiff. I'm sure I'll be okay, though."

"That's just in case, girl, and don't be afraid to call him. Well, I'm tired and have to catch a plane tomorrow for that long flight home. You coming?"

"Nah. Not right now," Marisa said as she continued staring at the fire. "I'm going to sit for a few more minutes."

"Okay, good night, girl. See you in the morning." Tiffany walked into the bedroom. "Oh, you *are* going to the airport to see me off, right?"

"Of course, you dweeb."

Tiffany walked back to the bedroom door. "Oh, it's like that? You gonna call me a dweeb?"

Marisa turned towards her. "Be thankful I didn't call you something else."

Tiffany walked towards the couch, tauntingly.

"Stop, Tiff," Marisa said with a warning in her tone.

They both laughed as she returned to the bedroom.

"Hey, where are the bed sheets? Or are we sleeping on a naked mattress tonight?"

Marisa chuckled. "No, look in the department store bags sitting in the closet."

"Oh, these are beautiful, Marisa," she said, pulling a duvet from the bag. "You got a little taste, huh?"

"I do." Marisa chuckled as she turned back towards the fire. "I do, indeed.

Ryan arrived early to pick up the girls for the airport. Marisa had curled up by the fireplace and was still asleep when the doorbell rang. He continued knocking and calling out to the girls. The knock startled Marisa. She sprang up to sitting position on the floor. Tiffany hearing the knocking opened the bedroom door.

"My goodness. I overslept?" she said as she hurried to open the door for Ryan.

Marisa raised up from the floor. The light from the sun rushed in through the front door.

"I see you ladies must have stayed up most of the night. Girl talk?"

Tiffany hugged him then headed back towards the living room. "No, I left Marisa sitting on the floor and went to bed. I must have slept pretty hard; must have been the new bed," she chuckled.

"Okay, what's your excuse, Marisa?"

Eyes closed, she laid her head on the back of the sofa. "I don't know, Ryan, I guess I was more tired than I thought."

Tiffany glanced at the clock on the nightstand. "Shoot! Come on, girl! Get up! I've got to be at the airport in less than two hours," she said, sprinting to the bathroom.

"I'm up, Tiff. I'm just so tired and I don't feel very well, either."

Tiffany stopped and went back to where Marisa was sitting. "What's wrong?" She felt her forehead with the back of her hand. "You do feel a bit warm. 'Course that could be because you slept by the fire on this dang floor."

Marisa leaned forward. "Yeah, I guess."

"Not to sound insensitive, ladies, but Tiff, babe, you don't have that long. Chop, chop." Ryan clapped his hands in an effort to get the girls moving. He loaded Tiffany's luggage into the car while she and Marisa finished dressing.

"All ready, Rissa?" Tiffany started walking towards the door.

"Yes, all ready," she replied, walking from the kitchen with a coffee cup in her hand.

"Well, lets go, girl."

Marisa placed the cup on the counter and headed for the door behind her. In the beginning the ride was fairly quiet. Ryan slowly reached over to hold Tiffany's hand. He interlocked his fingers with hers.

"I'm really going to miss you, you know."

Tiffany smiled. "Yeah, me too."

"So, what are you going to do while I'm gone?" she asked inquisitively. She wondered if the time they would be apart would change anything between the two of them. "I mean, I know how long distance relationships can be. If people don't see one another for a while sometimes things change..."

"You ever heard that saying about absence making the heart grow fonder?" Ryan asked her.

"Yes, I've heard the saying."

"Well, not gonna happen," he said playfully.

Tiffany punched him in the arm. "Ryan!"

"Okay, okay. I'm kidding."

"What? What's wrong?" Marisa had been asleep in the back seat, but awakened at the sound of their laughter.

"Nothing. Go back to sleep."

Marisa stretched. "Are we almost there?" she said through a yawn as she peered ahead between the seats.

"Yes, just about fifteen minutes away," Ryan said looking at the clock on the dashboard. "So, are you feeling any better?" he asked.

"Um, yeah. I think so. I was just so tired."

"You know, I'm not going to be here for a month or so, so don't go getting sick over here all by yourself."

"I'll be fine, girl. You're such a mother hen."

Tiffany clucked like a chicken. "Yes, I am honey and don't you forget it."

"Seriously, I will make sure to check on you when I get back to the states. We can email and Skype."

"Well, here we are," Ryan said as they pulled into the parking garage of the airport.

"Oh, we're here," Tiffany said as she saw a plane taxiing onto the runway.

They all exited the car. Ryan grabbed the luggage and placed it on the sidewalk near the check-in station. Marisa hugged Tiffany.

"I'm so going to miss you."

"Me too, girl. Take care till I get back and make sure to stay in touch." She snapped her fingers. "Oh, I put the cleaning supplies in the laundry room on that lil' skinny brown stand."

"Oh, we had some left?"

"Yes. Now don't forget, Marisa. You know you can be absent-minded and end up buying something you don't need."

"I won't forget, Tiff."

Marisa gave her one last hug. She then walked away to give Ryan and Tiffany some time alone.

"Happy trails, kiddo."

"Thanks, Ryan. You know I will miss you most of all. This has been such an amazing trip, and meeting you, well, it's just been the icing on the cake for me."

"I feel the same, Tiffany. I hope when you get back we can pick up where we left off," he said as he drew her towards him. He kissed her lips gently then pulled her closer. "You're an amazing woman, you know that?"

"Yes, I do," she said as Ryan gazed into her eyes.

"Get a room!" Marisa said, noticing their outward show of affection.

They all laughed.

A voice rang out from the airport intercom. *"International flight 1-6-5-8 for the U.S. now boarding at gate four."*

"Ohhh, that's my flight."

Ryan was still embracing her. Marisa walked up behind them, and cleared her throat.

"Excuse me, love birds, unless she's planning on catching another flight you'd better turn my girl loose so she can board." Marisa rocked back and forth on her heels, her hands clasped behind her back.

Tiffany backed away from Ryan, smiling as she turned towards Marisa. "Love you, girl," she said, giving her a quick hug before boarding.

"Yeah, me too."

"I'm going to really miss you guys."

"Last call for Delta International flight 1-6-5-8, now boarding for the U.S." the voice echoed once again from the speaker.

"Okay, I got to go. See you guys when I get back."

Tiffany ran up to Ryan and hugged him once more before running towards the boarding gate. She turned, walking down the corridor to her flight while waving. She then blew them a kiss and waved goodbye once more. A moment later, Ryan and Marisa headed back to the car.

"I'm going to miss my girl. Thank you, Ryan."

"Thanks? For what?"

"For making Tiffany's trip such a pleasure."

"Oh, nah. The pleasure was all mine, trust me."

"So, you really like my girl, huh?"

He opened the car door for her. "You know, Marisa, I've dated before, of course, but Tiffany, well, she's different. She's smart. She knows what direction she wants her life to go and she's funny as hell…and beautiful."

Marisa could hear the sincerity in his voice. "Yeah. She's an awesome friend, too."

Ryan closed her door, and walked around to the driver's side. Marisa watched him, suddenly curious as to his past relationships. She remembered what his sister had started to share at the club the other night. For a few minutes neither Marisa nor Ryan said a word as they drove back to her place.

"Oh, there's Tiffany's flight!" she said, pointing towards the plane that was taking off from the runway.

"Yeah, I wish her safe travels. You know I've gone to the states before, and I tell you, I had the worst jet lag." Ryan tried glancing at the plane once more as it ascended into the air. "I'm really going to miss her."

Knowing he was serious made Marisa become more inquisitive. She didn't want Tiffany to be hurt and felt, as her best friend, she had to know.

"Um, Ryan…" she began a bit hesitant, but then shook off any apprehensions and continued, "…your sister was telling me about your last relationship. She didn't go into any specifics, but referred to a girl you had dated, well, in her exact words, were engaged to. May I ask what happened between the two of you?"

Ryan glanced at Marisa. For almost fifteen minutes he didn't respond. No acknowledgement, no answer, just silence. She started to feel a little uncomfortable, and wondered if she had crossed the line by asking him about his past. Not knowing what to say next she turned and looked out the window. The buildings seemed to pass by in slow motion as she tried to ward off the awkwardness that filled the car.

Pulling up to her apartment, they both sat there for a moment without saying a word. "Um, thank you, Ryan," she said, grabbing the handle, on the verge of opening the door to get out. "I guess I will see you later—"

"She died," Ryan said just as Marisa opened the car door.

She turned towards him, a look of shock on her face. "I'm sorry, what did you say?" her hand still holding the handle.

"Her name was Letha. She was killed."

Marisa paused, not knowing what to say. "I'm so sorry, Ryan. I didn't mean to pry."

"No, it's okay."

She didn't know if she should but Marisa was able to squeeze out her next question. "So, if you don't mind me asking, how did she die? I mean, if this is too painful you don't have to talk about it. Really, it's okay, really."

Ryan sat staring straight ahead.

"I can see it's still painful for you and—"

"No, I've come to terms with it," he said interrupting her. "She, um...she was getting off work one night—I had been working a lot of hours with late night property showings, scores of paperwork—and she wanted to see me."

He paused for a moment. "I was still at the office when I told her I would meet her at one of the local restaurants close to where she was." His hands tightened on the steering wheel as he took a deep breath.

"I got so caught up in what I was doing, and forgot. Over an hour had passed before I remembered I was to meet her. I called, but she didn't answer. I kept calling while I drove to the restaurant. When I got there she wasn't there. She had left.

I figured she'd gotten angry and left to go home. I could never get an answer. Finally, her mother called. She was hysterical. I knew something was terribly wrong. My heart sank in my chest. I could hear her mother say she's gone, *'my Letha is gone'.*

I felt like I was in a black tunnel with no end. My head started spinning. I pulled off onto the side of the road and I just sat there, motionless, numb. I don't know how long I was there. I could hear her mother's voice over and over in my head..."

"Oh, my God, Ryan!" Marisa placed her hand across her chest as she listened in disbelief.

He continued, "She had been working long nights and had gotten in her car to meet me at the restaurant. She fell asleep behind the wheel and hit an oncoming car. She was killed instantly."

Marisa's eyes filled with tears. "I am so, so sorry, Ryan," she said empathetically.

"Its okay. It's been two years now. It still hurts but I know I've got to keep going. Every morning I wake I know in my heart I have to keep breathing and put one foot in front of the other." He looked at Marisa. "Letha was an amazing person. I know she would have wanted me to."

They both sat in silence. The sound of a car passed by them. You could hear the tires of the slow moving car against the cobblestone street. In the distance the faint sound of music drifted from the little tavern that sat a couple of blocks away.

"Thank you for sharing such a sensitive part of your life, Ryan. You know, I guess things happen sometimes that's out of our control. We don't always understand why and it's hard to talk about them. Trust me, I know," she said as the thought of her rape entered her mind. "Depending on what it is, you just kinda hold it inside."

"Yeah, but you know what I've learned, Marisa?" He turned to look at her. "I've learned that no matter how tragic a thing is, you have to find peace and some form of closure. You need to talk about it. You need to face it head on. It's a fact that things will happen in life that you may have no control over and may never understand. But you can't let it take your power. You have to find a way to keep going, to be strong. If you don't, that thing will stifle you. You can't truly live, because that *thing* will always be there, haunting you and interrupting your life."

Marisa was thoughtful, his words resonated inside her very core. Looking at him, she slowly nodded her head in agreement.

"I guess I'd better let you go," she said as she opened the car door. Ryan got out and hurried to the other side. He held it for her. "Thank you, Ryan. Your words were enlightening. I guess we all have our challenges to face."

He smiled. "Yeah, I guess we do. See you later."

Marisa climbed the few steps to her apartment. Unlocking her door she turned to see Ryan standing outside of the car. "Is something wrong?"

"Nope. Just making sure you get inside safely," he said, motioning for her to go on inside.

"You know, Tiff is lucky to have run into you, Ryan." She smiled as she closed the door, and locked it. She stood there for a few minutes with her back leaned against the door, his words still echoing in her mind. She knew she had been blocking the night of the rape from her thoughts. And the numbing thought of Matt being somewhere in London didn't make it any easier.

5
The Brittle Steps We Take

The next day would be Marisa's first day on her new job. She didn't know what to expect and felt a bit anxious as she dressed. She had to walk a block up the street to the bus stop. She pulled out the refill pass that Glenna had given her at the realty office. Standing at the bus stop, she sighed as she looked up and down the street.

Gosh, I feel like I want to barf. I'm so nervous. I'm so far away from my friends and family. What was I thinking taking this job? Wait, Marisa, calm down. She took a deep breath. *You'll be fine. You'll be just fine.*

Finally, the bus pulled up to the sidewalk. She could smell the fumes that seeped from its exhaust system really strong. The mechanisms made a hissing sound like that of a snake as the steps lowered to sidewalk level.

The driver smiled as Marisa stepped onto the bus. "Good morning, ma'am."

"Good morning," she replied, swiping her card. "Is this bus going to twenty-third Bank Street?"

"No, not quite. This bus will go as far as High Street. From there you will need to catch the D7. That will take you on to twenty-third."

"Oh, Okay. Thank you."

Marisa walked to the back of the bus as it slowly pulled off. It was nearly full so she chose to stand, holding onto the leather bus-strap above her head. She watched the screen just to the right of the driver's head. The next stop appeared consecutively as riders tugged the pull-cords to get off at their destinations.

Marisa's thoughts drifted for a while. This was going to be her first day on a new job and she didn't know what to expect. She wondered if she would make a good impression. Being the new kid on the block, to Marisa, meant all eyes would be on her, especially the boss's.

"Next stop High Street." The driver's voice came across the bus's intercom system. The scrolling marquee quickly flipped back into focus as Marisa came out of her daydream.

"High Street," Marisa said to herself. She tugged the pull-cord for her stop, and the driver pulled over.

"Have a good day."

"Oh, you too, sir." Marisa smiled as she exited the bus. She waited for the next one to arrive, nervously biting her bottom lip as she rolled her right foot from side to side.

"Um, you're going to ruin those beautiful shoes."

Marisa turned to see where the voice was coming from. She pointed to herself. "Oh, are you speaking to me?" she said to the woman sitting on the bench.

"Yes, I am. I happened to notice that nervous twitch you have with your foot, which is the reason I said you're going to ruin those beautiful shoes. You know rolling them from side to side like that..."

Marisa looked down at her shoes. She chuckled. "Oh, I'm starting a new job today. I guess I'm a bit nervous."

"Oh, really? Where?"

At first Marisa hesitated. The woman was a stranger and lately she wasn't too fond of strangers. "Oh, no worries. I'm not a serial killer or anything."

"It's, um, with a marketing firm on Bank Street."

"Bank Street? That's where I'm going. What's the name of the firm?"

"The Brusselton Marketing Firm."

"What?!"

Excitedly, Samantha stood up from the bench where she was sitting. She was about five-feet eight in height. Her red curly hair was pulled back in a loose bun. A small number of freckles dotted her oval face. And she wore a dark salmon colored pant suit that flattered her small slender frame.

"By the way, my name is Sam Risqué. Actually it's Samantha...Sam for short." She extended her hand to shake Marisa's. "Oh and don't mind the last name." She chuckled. "That's not a true representation of who I am. So, you said Brusselton, did you?"

"I'm Marisa...Marisa Webb. And yes, on Bank street."

"Well, believe it or not, that's where I'm headed. I work there."

A look of surprise came across Marisa's face. "Oh really? For how long?"

Just as Samantha was about to answer the bus pulled up. The door swung open and the driver looked at them expectantly. "All aboard, ladies. Running a bit behind," he said with a sense of urgency.

"Come on, Marisa. Let's get on before he pulls off and leaves us standing here." They laughed as they looked for seats. Samantha spotted a couple of empty seats near the middle of the bus. "Come on, we'll grab these." When they sat down Sam continued the conversation.

"So I've been working with Brusselton for nearly five years. It's really a great company. Are you just coming aboard?"

"Actually, I am," Marisa said as she adjusted in her seat. "I came over from the U.S. I graduated college about three weeks ago and flew straight over here to start with Brusselton's."

"Wow! All the way from the states? That's amazing. You must come with high recommendations."

"Well, I don't know about that," Marisa turned a shade of red from embarrassment.

"Oh, stop being so modest. So, what will you be doing?"

"Um, I'm going to be working as one of the foreign exchange liaisons."

"That's great! That means we will be working pretty closely together."

"Really?"

Samantha's proclamation made her feel a bit more comfortable, feeling as if she had already developed an ally.

"So, what is it that you do, Sam?"

"Actually, I'm a part of the research and development team. We seek out and try to partner with companies we feel fit the scope of where Brusselton's is trying to go in the financial arena."

The bus came to a stop a block from the Brusselton building. The street was already filled with people scampering from restaurants and coffee shops into adjacent corporate buildings along the street. Car horns blared while taxi cabs rushed off to their next destination.

"London is such a beautiful and exciting place," Marisa said as she looked up at the high rise buildings.

"Come on, we can cross here. Yes, it is pretty amazing. Course when you live in a place, you don't quite appreciate it the way someone who doesn't. Know what I mean?"

Marisa shook her head in agreement. A horn blew, startling her just as they reached the sidewalk.

"Now, that's an everyday occurrence, Marisa. Some people, just like in America, can be jerks, you know. You'll get used to it quite quickly here, I'm sure. Well, we still have about forty minutes," Sam said looking down at her watch. "You drink coffee?"

"Uh, yes."

"Good, because there's a nice little coffee shop just there," Samantha pointed to a little red-faced building. "They have the best varieties in coffee. I go there often, seeing as though I'm a coffee-holic."

They laughed as they walked through the door, the little bell connected to it jingling softly above their heads.

"What will you have, Marisa?"

"I'll have a, uuuhh-mm…a caramel latte."

Sam turned to the man standing behind the counter.

"Hello, two medium caramel lattes, please." They stood there talking as they waited for their drinks.

"Two caramel lattes!" A voice rang out from behind the counter.

When the two of them finally got their coffees, they took a seat at a table near the shop's slightly tinted window. Marisa looked out and watched as people hurried in one direction or the other as she sipped on her coffee.

"So, how are the people at Brusselton's? I mean, like."

Sam laughed. "You don't have to explain what you mean," she said smiling. "I'll say this: we do have a few slackers. As a matter of fact I think one of them will be in the department where you're going." Samantha thought for a moment. "Let me see, oh okay, there is this one who you will recognize straight away. I call her *Ms. Large and In Charge*. She wants to run things and can be somewhat of a bully at times. You just have to know how to handle her."

Samantha continued giving Marisa the staffing profiles as they sipped their lattes, passing the time. "Then there's *Miss Squeaky Sneaky*. She's the one that will come across really innocent, but, well, you get what I'm saying. Oh! Then there is *The Pleaser*. Now I will say she's sweet, but she will as soon throw you under the bus to save face with the rest of the co-workers. Trust me, you will know them all when you see them." Sam glanced at her watch again. "Oh! Time to go. How time flies when you're discussing co-workers."

Samantha and Marisa burst into laughter as they grabbed their belongings and headed out the door.

They walked into the grey-faced brick building. A round service desk sat to the right of the elevators. Receptionists answered phones and ushered in clients for meetings. Two flights of stairs veered off and up to the left and to the right of the large atrium.

You could see the pale blue sky with soft white puffs of clouds drifting by through the skylight of the building. Just below were three elevator doors where people were waiting for the next one to open up.

"So, we have to go to the sixth floor." Sam hurried Marisa towards an opening elevator door. "We can take this one." A few others scampered onto the elevator as the door began to close.

"Wait! Wait!"

Sam could see someone waving their hand. She hit the button to stop the door from closing.

"Ohh! Good morning, good morning!" The lady said a bit winded as she got on the elevator. "Thank you."

"You're welcome, bobble."

Marisa looked at Sam. Her eyes bugged as she remembered their talk in the coffee shop.

"Huh?" The lady said as she turned around.

"I said *good morning*."

"Oh, it's you, Samantha. How are you?"

"Oh, I'm good, Pen. Ready for this day to get started."

Marisa smiled at Samantha.

People exited the elevator one floor after the other. Finally, reaching their floor the ladies walked out into a large open space. Another round service desk stood near the middle of the floor. Marisa panned the entire space, her eyes stopping at one of the walls. The name *Brusselton's Inc.* graced one of the enclosures in large silver letters that glistened from the reflection of the sun through the building's skylight.

Sam walked up to the desk with Marisa. "Hi, Eva. This is Marisa."

The woman smiled.

"Oh my. I never got your last name."

"Webb. Marisa Webb."

"She need to see personnel."

"Sure thing." The woman picked up the phone and began to dial.

"Well, I will catch up with you a bit later, Marisa. Got an early morning meeting, and still have to do my makeup."

"Sure, um, absolutely." Marisa shook Sam's hand. She watched as her new friend walked down the hall.

"Miss Webb?" Marisa turned towards the receptionist who was now standing beside her. "Come with me, please."

She followed the receptionist down towards a glass office door that read *Brusselton Foreign Exchange Servicing*.

The room was small with high-walled cubicle offices. Again, Marisa followed the receptionist down the aisle towards another office with a glass door. Written on the entrance was the name *Brandon Kubrick*. The receptionist walked in and headed toward another desk.

"Miss Webb to see Mr. Kubrick. He will assist you from here. Welcome aboard."

With that the receptionist went back to her desk. The man walked over to a door and knocked softly. A voice from the other side gave permission to enter.

"Hello, Mr. Kubrick. Miss Marisa Webb to see you."

"Send her in."

He was an older, stocky gentleman with a receding hairline; his salt and pepper hair was neatly combed back. Marisa could tell from the plaques on the wall that he had been with the company for a long time and was very accomplished educationally.

"I've heard really good things about you, young lady. Have a seat." He nodded toward a chair in front of his desk. "Thank you, Morris."

The receptionist nodded his head and smiled as he slowly closed the door behind him.

"So, have you settled into our little city?" The man looked at Marisa, smiling. He somehow reminded her of her father, and the way he used to be before the affairs started.

"Well, sir, I'm adjusting pretty well."

"Uh-huh," Mr Kubrick grunted. "What about a place to live?"

Now, he was really beginning to sound like her father.

"I found an apartment. Getting settled in."

"Good, good. Well, you came with a high recommendation from your school, young lady. I believe you are going to do well here."

Marisa smiled. "Thank you, sir."

Mr. Kubrick got up from his seat and began to pace near the window. "I've been here for thirty-five years and I tell ya, it hasn't always been easy, but I put forth my best efforts because they gave me a chance. This will be the chance of a lifetime for you, Miss Webb. I picked you because I believed what I saw in your recommendation letter."

"Thank you, Mr. Kubrick. This is by far the greatest opportunity I could have—"

"No, nooo," Mr. Kubrick interrupted. "There were better opportunities out there, young lady. It's all about what you do with the opportunity you decide to take. The opportunity is in you to prove that you are the best one for the job."

Marisa smiled and nodded her head in agreement with him.

"Welp, I've talked enough," the man chuckled.

"Well, thank you for your faith and confidence in me, Mr. Kubrick. I won't let you down."

He clasped his hands behind his back. "You know, you remind me of my daughter. She had a very bright and promising future. She was a hard worker. Yeah, a pretty bright future..." he appeared to have drifted off in his thoughts. "She's no longer with us," he said, giving Marisa a somber smile.

"Oh, I'm so sorry, Mr Kubrick."

"Yeah, she was diagnosed with cancer a few years ago. That aggressive kind, you know. We lost her the winter of, uuhhh, two-thousand and five."

Marisa sat quietly.

"Listen at me going off course here. Well, young lady, I'm going to introduce you to the rest of the team, then we will get you settled."

The two of them walked out of the office. Marisa met the entire staff and was shown her cubicle. It had a beautiful picturesque view of the city outside. She could see the people going about their day down below.

Wow, I'm really here. Here in London. This is surreal. Marisa smiled to herself just as a faint knock sounded on the opening of her cubicle.

"Hi, Marisa?"

"Yes," she said, reaching out to shake the woman's hand. "I'm Marisa."

"I'm Beverly. I just wanted to personally introduce myself." The woman sat down in the extra office chair. "I wanted to let you know that if you need anything or require any help, just let me know. I've been in this area for seven years so I know a lot about the procedures and contacts and, well, I can be a wealth of knowledge for you. I just wanted to let you know."

"Oh, well," Marisa cleared her throat. "Thank you, um, Beverly, right?" she smiled as she thought this must be the person Sam had warned her about. "I will certainly keep that in mind."

The woman stood up and pointed to her cubicle. "I sit right over there, right by Mr. Kubrick's office."

Marisa peeped her head out of the cubicle and looked in the direction Beverly was pointing. "Oh, okay. I will definitely remember that."

The woman walked down the aisle and disappeared into her cubicle.

"Well, that was weird," Marisa muttered as she pushed her chair back to her desk.

The day flew by and Marisa found herself on her way back to catch the bus before she knew what happened.

"Hey, Hey!" A voice came from across the street. It was Sam. Marisa smiled as she waved back. It was good seeing a familiar face. "So, how was your first day?"

"It was great...and interesting."

Sam looked at her, a curious look on her face. "Interesting?" The word Marisa chose warranted her suspicions, and she chuckled. "You must have met *Miss Large and In Charge.*"

Marisa laughed. "I kinda think I did." She and Sam laughed again.

"Let me give you my address and phone number." Sam dug into her purse for a pen and paper. "Maybe we can get together for happy hour, or something."

"Oh, that sounds great. My best friend just flew back to the states over the weekend and won't be back for a few weeks. It would be nice to have someone to kinda hang out with. You actually remind me a lot of her," Marisa was saying as she reached for the paper that held Sam's contact information.

The bus back to Camden was a block away when she looked across the street. Leaning against a lamp post she thought she recognized the person standing there. *Matt?* she thought to herself. Her heart began to race inside her chest. A feeling of near-panic overwhelmed her. As if in a trance, she moved dangerously close to the edge of the curb trying to get a better look.

"Marisa? Marisa." Sam looked across the street as she wondered what had the girl so captivated. "What are you looking at?"

Marisa walked closer and closer to the edge of the curb. She didn't see the bus just a few feet away. She just *had* to know if it was him. She had to see if it was Matt. The bus drew closer just as she stepped off the curb.

"Marisa!" Sam grabbed her by the arm and pulled her back, and she immediately she came back to her senses. "What the —? Girl!" Sam placed her hand on her chest. "I guess you don't want to work at Brusselton's for very long, do you?"

"Huh?" Marisa seemed as if she had just been snapped out of a trance. She walked to the front of the bus, looking around it to see if the person was still standing there.

Sam looked as well. "What in the name of all things cute are you looking at?"

"I—I thought I saw someone I knew."

"Well, if they were there," Sam looked again, "they must have gotten on the bus that's pulling off because there's no one there now." Sam pulled out her bus pass. "We're going to be walking home if we don't get on this one."

Marisa pulled her own pass from the side pocket of her jacket. "Yeah," she said. Still feeling shaken, she sat quietly as the sound of the bus's engine seemed distant in her thoughts.

"You've been pretty quiet ever since we got on the bus. Are you sure you're okay? You almost seemed spooked back there."

"I, um, I just thought I saw someone."

"Yes, like someone you'd prefer not to see, it seems."

Marisa smiled nervously. "Just someone from college that I'd rather not bump into." She looked out the window as she twiddled her fingers.

"Hmmm, old boyfriend, I gather?"

Marisa looked at her. "No, no, not at all."

"Well, why does he make you so nervous?"

Instead of answering, she tugged the pull-cord above her for the next stop. "This is where I get off." She got up from her seat and held onto the railing over her shoulder.

"Really? Why, I live about four blocks up this street." Sam smiled.

"Well, that's my place right there." She pointed to the building with the hanging plants and a small bed of chrysanthemums.

"What a beautiful place."

"I will definitely invite you over sometime."

Sam smiled. "That would be nice."

"Oh, and thank you for taking me under your wing and showing me around today."

"It was my pleasure, Marisa. Well, see you tomorrow."

"Sure thing." She got off the bus, and waved to her new friend. Sam waved back. "See you tomorrow."

Marisa hurried inside the apartment. She slammed and locked the door behind her. Leaning against it, she stood there for a while as thoughts of *that night* rushed through her mind.

I can't keep going like this. I'm a nervous wreck.

She walked to the bathroom. Placing her hands under the running water, she gently patted her face with warm water. Suddenly her cell phone rang. Startled, she turned quickly, bracing herself against the sink. Realizing it was her phone she took a deep breath. "Calm down, girl. Pull yourself together," she said aloud as she hurried to answer it.

"Hello?"

"Hey girl, what 'cha doing?"

It was Tiffany. She was back in the states. "So how's things? Did you meet any new and interesting people today at, wait, what's the name again? Brussel Sprouts?"

Marisa could hear Tiffany snort on the other end of the phone. She chuckled herself. "Oh, you have jokes, huh? It's Brusselton's."

"Oh, yeah, that's right," she giggled. "So how did it go?"

"Actually, it was really nice. I ran into this girl, Samantha—Sam, for short. She kind of gave me the heads up on a few people in the office and showed me around. She lives, like, a few blocks up the street."

"Really? Oh, she trying to move in on BFF territory, huh?"

"Really, Tiffany?"

"Girl, I'm just playing, lighten up. Matter of fact you know you're not fooling me, right?"

"What are you talking about?"

"Marisa, how many times do I have to say how well I know you? What's up? I can hear it in your voice. What happened since I've been gone?"

She paused as she tried to gather her thoughts. "I—I thought I saw Matt at the bus stop across the street today, just a block up from where I work."

"What? Like, was it him for sure?"

"I don't know. All I remember is looking across the street when Sam and I were waiting for the bus. I saw this guy leaning against a pole, but I didn't get a good look because the bus came and blocked my view."

"Marisa, I really think you need to get some protection."

"I don't like guns, Tiffany. I get nervous at the thought of them." She paused. "Hold on…" She placed the phone on the bed and hurried to the bathroom.

Leaning over the sink just in time, her stomach heaved up her lunch from earlier that day. Grabbing a hand towel from the linen closet she soaked it then patted her mouth. She stood over the sink for a minute holding the towel across her face. Then after she felt stable, she returned to the phone.

"Hello…hello? Tiff?"

"Yeah, girl. You okay?"

"Yeah, I think with all that's happened today I'm just exhausted and my nerves are on, like, steroids or something."

"Well, I'll be back in a few weeks. I can bring a gun with me, you know. I might get held up by customs, but—"

"No, Tiffany! You play too much," she said as they both laughed. "I'll get some pepper spray or something."

"In all seriousness, I just want you to be safe."

"I know, Tiff."

"I spoke with Ryan today."

"Oh yeah?" she laid back on the bed and placed the cool, wet towel across her forehead. "How's he doing?"

"He's fine. He said he would check on you for me."

"Tiff, I'm fine…really I am."

"You don't sound like it to me."

"I'm just tired, you know, first day on a new job, catching buses, seeing ghosts of college past…yadda, yadda, yadda."

"Mmm-hhhmm, sure. You just take care and think about what I said about you talking to someone and getting some protection." Her voice raised another octave. "You hear me, Marisa?"

"Sure, Tiff."

"Alright, I've gotta go, girl. You know these international calls aren't cheap," she laughed.

"Okay, girl. Thank you so much for calling. I miss you."

"Yeah, yeah, miss you, too. Okay, talk soon."

"Give your mom my love."

"Will do, Rissa. Smooches."

Marisa continued lying on the bed. She stared up at the ceiling, listening to the dial tone until it began to beep. Hitting the *off* button, she let the phone drop to the bed.

Maybe Tiffany's right. Maybe I should get a gun. Wait! I've never fired or even touched a gun in my life! Besides, I could never shoot anyone.

The thought of taking someone's life sent chills down her spine. She sat up on the side of the bed and placed the now slightly warmed towel around the back of her neck, and sighed.

Why? Why did this have to happen to me? I feel like I'm having a nervous breakdown.

She made her way back to the bathroom to cool the towel once more. She held it under the running water. Squeezing away the excess, she raised her head and looked at herself in the mirror.

But I can't keep going like this. Maybe I do need to— she stopped. *No!* she thought, shaking her head. *I can't. I can't tell a complete stranger about that. Besides, the sooner I forget it ever happened...the better.*

Marisa walked back to the bedroom. She flopped down on the edge of the bed, placing the towel over her eyes.

I'm so ashamed. Why me? Was it something I said? Was it—was it something I did?

She closed her eyes as she fell back against the bed. Pounding the mattress with the side of her fist she tried to make sense of it all. The memories again seeped into her mind. She could still remember the woodsy smell of her assailant's cologne as vividly as if it were present even now. Suddenly, she stopped and opened her eyes. She slowly raised from the bed and looked towards her door.

What was that? Marisa wondered as she quietly got to her feet and walked towards the door, looking around for anything she could use to protect herself. She grabbed the scissors from the dresser she had been using to cut open boxes. Her heart pounding in her chest, she wondered if she had locked the front door after coming home.

"Who's there?" She called out, but there was no answer.

Cautiously she peeked out the bedroom, and looked towards the living room. She could tell it was locked. Then she looked towards the kitchen. Holding the scissors in front of her she looked around with every step she took. Suddenly she heard the sound again coming from the laundry room.

Stopping, she said, "Who's there?"

Sweat poured from her forehead. Placing the scissors in her left hand, she slowly reached for the handle on the laundry room door. Snatching it back, she jumped just as a falling bag of cleaning supplies crashed to the floor.

"I'm going to kill her!" Marisa said as she remembered Tiffany telling her where she had placed the cleaning supplies. She picked up the items that had scattered across the floor, and placed them back in the bag. On the floor beside the washer was a better place to set it.

For a moment there was a sigh of relief as Marisa thought to herself. *Wait until I tell Tiff I forgot,* she stood there looking at the bag and then burst into tears. "I want my life back," she said, sobbing. "I just want to live again. How dare he take my peace of mind away from me. How dare he take my security!"

Marisa grabbed the scissors she had lain on the counter. Holding them with both hands she sunk them into the counter.

"How dare he!"

Overwhelmed with a flood of emotions, Marisa sank down the counter to the floor. What was only a few minutes seemed like hours as she sat in silence.

She soon made her way back to her feet, looking down the hallway to the living room. The hall seemed longer than she remembered as she slowly walked down it. She checked the lock and the windows to make sure they were secured.

I think I'm going to have an alarm system put in, Marisa thought to herself as she headed back to the bedroom.

Exhausted, she pulled back the bed covers, and brought them over her head when she managed to guide her weary bones underneath them. Pulling the covers back slightly, she looked over at her bedroom door. Staring at it for a moment she decided to get up and lock it.

There, she thought. *I won't ever make that mistake again.*

Two weeks had passed and Marisa's name was already buzzing around Brusselton's.

"Marisa! Marisa!" It was Sam. "Whooo, I need to work out," she said winded from the fast pace she was using to catch up.

Marisa laughed. "You and me both, Sam."

"So, you headed out to lunch?"

"Um, no. I'm actually headed out to an appointment." She looked at Sam as they walked out of the building.

"Appointment? Oh, okay. Well, I hear the talk around the office is that the boss is really impressed with the way you've been performing. Congratulations on snagging that Bloomis account. Way to go, lady."

"Actually, it was a team effort so…"

Sam started to laugh. "Girl, you and your modesty. That was a major deal. Take your credit and run. It's not often that happens with a newbie in the company."

Marisa smiled. "Thank you, Sam. I appreciate it."

"Well, gotta run. You go to your appointment, I'm going to get some lunch. TGIF, girl! I'll catch up with you later." Sam waved goodbye as she hurried down the sidewalk in the opposite direction.

Marisa looked at her phone. "Okay, lets see…" She plugged the address of her destination into her cell. *Oh, darn, it's like two blocks away.* Marisa sped up her pace. *I don't want to be late*, she continued down the street. *Oh, there it is.*

At the push of the button, the cars came to a halt, and she hurried across the street. The sign on the entrance of the building read *"Corning Medical Group"*.

"Hello, I have an appointment with Dr. Dana Corning, please."

The receptionist gave Marisa a clipboard. "Fill these forms out, please, to the best of your knowledge."

"Um, okay." Marisa took the clipboard and walked over to a nearby chair to complete them.

Thirty long minutes passed, making Marisa glance at her watch. *I guess doctor's offices are the same no matter what country you're—*

"Marisa Webb?" The back office nurse called as she opened the door. Marisa got up and followed her to the examination room. "Hello, Miss Webb. I'm sorry for the wait, the doctor had an emergency delivery call earlier. She's back in the office now. Here's a gown. If you will go ahead and change into this I will be back to take your vitals." The nurse smiled as she closed the door behind her.

Marisa changed into the light blue gown. She pulled it around her body as she sat in a padded chair near the door. Soon there was a faint knock as the nurse walked back in to start the process.

"Okay, Miss Webb. You can have a seat on the exam table. Dr. Corning is reviewing your medical summary and will be right in."

"Okay. Thank you."

She sat on the exam table, and nervously looked around the room. Her eyes darted from one article to the next on the pale beige walls. Her inquisitive gaze landed on the model of a womb with a baby turned towards the birthing canal. Then the door opened again for the second time.

"Hello, Miss Webb?" The doctor looked at the clipboard that held the papers Marisa had filled out earlier.

"Yes." Marisa reached out to shake Dr. Corning's hand as it came towards her.

"So, what brings you in today?"

"I, ummm, have been feeling really weird lately."

"Weird?" the doctor smiled.

"Yes. I just moved here from the states; just started a new job and it's been nonstop. I don't know…I think I'm just exhausted."

"That could be a possibility. Your vitals look good. I'm waiting on the results from your blood work and the urinalysis."

Just then the nurse knocked at the door, and walked into the room. "Here are the test results, Dr Corning."

The doctor looked over the reports. "Well, here is one of your problems." She looked up at Marisa. "You're anemic so we definitely need to get that taken care of. Let's see. Marisa, can you tell me when was your last period?"

She thought about it for a moment. "Um, I think over a month now. I'm not sure, I—."

"Okay, well let's do a cervical examine. If you'll go ahead and lie back…"

The nurse pulled out a drawer inside the examination table revealing some medical tools. "Okay, take a deep breath and relax."

Marisa took a deep breath as Dr. Corning picked up the speculum.

"Okay, we're going to take a look at your cervix, sweetie. Relax for me."

The procedure was over really quickly. Marisa sat on the exam table while Dr. Corning completed her chart. Her heart felt like it would burst from her chest as she waited for the doctor to finish.

"Well, you are anemic and I'm going to write you a prescription for that. And based on the other test we just ran and the enlargement of your cervix…it appears you are also pregnant."

Marisa sat motionless. The words of Dr. Corning seemed to echo from a long tunnel.

"I gather this is unexpected?"

Marisa nodded her head. She felt paralyzed.

"Well, Marisa, as a doctor, I can tell you that you do have options. I'm going to give you some information and in your leisure you can look it over. In the interim I want you to get the prescription filled so that you can start building your blood."

Dr. Corning left the room. Marisa's mind reeled with confusion as she began to get dressed. *This can't be real. This can't be happening to me,* her eyes filled with tears as she collapsed onto a chair. She covered her face. *Oh God! This can't be happening to me!*

The nurse walked in to give Marisa the information Dr. Corning had talked about. "Are you okay, Miss Webb?"

"Um, yes, yes."

"Do you need me to get you some water or—"

"No, I'm fine."

"Well, here is the prescription and here is the information on pregnancy and—"

"Yes, yes, thank you," taking the papers.

"If you have any questions here is the office information and hours."

"Thank you."

"Are you sure you're okay?"

"Yes." Marisa managed a slight smile as she walked out of the examination room.

The words of Dr. Corning played over and over in her head. She sat on the bench at the bus stop. Numb, she felt like she was having an out-of-body experience. Looking across the street, she stared at her reflection in the building window.

I'm pregnant? I'm pregnant from a freakin' stranger! From someone who took advantage of me!

She felt like screaming with everything inside of her as she repeatedly pounded her fist into her thigh.

After what felt like an eternity, the bus finally pulled up. Just when the door swung open, Marisa slowly raised from the bench and made her way on the bus for the ride home.

6
Crumbling Beneath Her Feet

The next morning Marisa lay motionless in her bed. She listened as cars slowly moved along the cobblestone street. The silence of the apartment gave way to the deafening words of Dr. Corning. A tear streamed down the side of her face, wetting the pillow beneath her head.

I can't keep this pregnancy. I can't. I've got to figure out what to do. Suddenly the phone rang. Marisa, startled from her thoughts, grabbed her cell phone. "Hello?"

"Hi. Marisa?"

"Um, yes."

"Ryan. How are you?"

"Wow. Hi, Ryan. It's been a few days. I didn't quite catch your voice."

He chuckled. "I was just calling to check on you. How's things?"

"Well, things are fine, just fine. Work is good. I'm finding my way around quite well. How about you? You heard from Tiffany?"

"Oh, yeah. I actually just got off the phone with her. She said she would be calling you later today."

"She did?"

"Yeah. She can't wait to get back and quite frankly, I can't wait to see her."

Marisa tried to sound upbeat. She didn't want Ryan to detect that anything was wrong. "I'm sure she feels the same way."

"Cool, I just wanted to reach out and make sure everything's okay in your part of the city."

"Oh, sure. Thank you so much for checking."

"No problem, it's my pleasure. It's been good talking with you. You have my number make sure you call if you need to."

"Sure thing, Ryan, thanks for calling."

"Absolutely. Well, bye for now."

"Bye, and thank you again."

Marisa let the phone drop beside her. As she raised up to sit on the edge of the bed, she noticed the brochures the nurse had given her on the night stand. Reaching over she grabbed the papers, closed her eyes and took a deep breath.

Slowly opening her eyes she began to read out loud. "Planned Parenthood. Abortion is the safe and legal way to end a pregnancy." Marisa paused and took another deep breath. "Learn if abortion is right for you. Abortion risks…"

The more she read, the more she felt overwhelming anxiety. Her mind was flooded with the echoes of *that night*, of her father's infidelities, her mother's passivity and the words of Dr. Corning. She thought about how her life had been altered by one selfish individual who had thought only of himself.

Marisa became enraged. She threw the papers at the wall. Angry, she got up and headed to her closet. Pulling out a yellow blouse she threw it on the bed then grabbed a pair of blue jeans from the dresser drawer. After dressing, she stormed out of the apartment.

She walked for what felt like hours, her eyes blinded by tears. Her mind and emotions were at a peak, and she was exhausted. She ended up at the tavern just down the street from her apartment. Sitting at the bar she grabbed the drink menu.

"What will it be, ma'am?"

Marisa pointed to one of the pictures on the menu. "I'll have this Bone Martini," she said hesitantly.

"Coming right up." The bartender left to mix her drink.

The music filled the room as people moved to the dance floor. Others sat in groups around the bar laughing, or immersed in conversation.

"Here you go, ma'am."

The bartender sat the drink down on a little white napkin in front of her. Marisa slowly raised the glass towards her mouth. In that same moment, the words of Dr. Corning echoed through her mind again:

"You're pregnant."

Marisa paused for a moment. *I'm not having this, this…*

She raised the glass to her lips again. Blocking out her thoughts she turned it up and drank until it was empty.

"Whoa..."

A voice came from behind her. Turning toward it, she saw Patrick standing with one hand on the counter top.

"Girl, I don't remember you drinking in college."

Surprised to see him, Marisa was speechless for a moment. "Um, yeah, I didn't really." She grabbed the white napkin from the counter and wiped her mouth as he sat down in the chair beside her.

"Weird seeing you here. You with someone?" he said staring at her.

"Yeah, I mean no, no. I'm not with anyone. I live up the street a ways."

"Oh, is that right?"

"Yeah, but enough about me. What are you doing here, Patrick?" Marisa looked to see if anyone was sitting alone, waiting for his return.

"I'm out here with a friend of mine. He, umm, he stepped outside with his girl to have a conversation."

"Is he acting a fool?"

Patrick laughed. "What makes you say that?"

"You know how you men are, always doing shit you have no business doing."

"Wait a minute," he laughed. "Where did that come from? Sure don't remember you using those kinds of words either."

"Guess I've changed."

"Changed? How so?" He leaned in closer to hear her answer.

"Um, well...a new job, away from my family, starting a new life. It's just a lot to handle."

Patrick leaned in closer. "Tell you a secret?"

"Another round, ma'am?"

Marisa looked at the bartender. "It's the weekend. Why not?"

"I'll have one of the same."

"Are you sure you can handle that?"

"I'm sure."

Just then a five-foot three brunette walked up behind Patrick. "Hey, ready to go?"

He turned around in the bar stool. "Um, yeah. Where's Greg?"

"I guess he's gone to the car."

"Oh, okay. Well, um, guess I'll see ya around."

"Yeah, sure," Marisa said as he raised up from the seat.

"Take it easy on the liquor. Things happen when people are drunk."

Marisa smiled. "I'm sure."

She watched as Patrick and the woman walked out the door. *Well, that was awkward,* she said to herself. *Must have been some kind of argument,* Marisa thought for a minute. *You know what? I have too much going on in my life to try and evaluate someone else's situation.*

She paid the bartender and placed a tip on the counter top. Walking out of the tavern, she looked up at the sky. The stars twinkled one after the other.

Humph! It's brighter out here than it is in there, Marisa giggled. She stood there for a minute. *Ooo, well I'm feeling kinda, let's see...Tiff would say, uummm, oh yeah, kinda cute.*

Marisa placed her hand over her mouth and giggled again. Slowly making her way up the dimly lit street, the cobblestones made it difficult for her to keep from stumbling in her inebriated state.

"Hey, baby! You want a ride?" A man said from a car that had slowed down next to her.

"No, thank you."

"Are you sure? Looks like you're going in the same direction as I am," the man chuckled as he hung his hand out the window.

"I said no!" Marisa took off her shoe and threw it towards the car. It landed in the back seat.

"You're crazy!" The guy yelled as he sped away.

Finally making it inside of her apartment in one piece, Marisa fell across the bed. *I just need some sleep. I'm tired. I'll get my shoe tomorrow.* And with that she drifted off.

Marisa was awakened by a faint vibration and buzzing sound. She raised her head to look around. Slowly she laid her head back on the bed face down. Again she felt the vibrations and could hear the buzzing sound.

"What?" She looked again. Her eyes landed on the cell phone she had left on the bed earlier that evening. The notification light pierced the still darkened room. Quickly, she reached for the phone.

"Oh my god…my head," Marisa said as she picked up the phone. "Hello, hello?"

The voice on the other end was faint.

"Hello? I can hardly hear you. Who's this?" Again the voice was faint. Puzzled, she looked at the phone. Realizing it was upside down, she dropped it on the bed as she tried to turn it around. "Oops. Hello? Hello?"

"Hello? Marisa?" It was Tiffany calling. "OMG! I've been calling you all evening. Where have you been? Are you okay?"

"Tiff, don't yell. My head is killing me."

"What? Are you sick? I mean, like, are you coming down with something?"

"No, no. I um, I went down to this little tavern down the street and, um, I think I'm drunk," she giggled. "I had too much to drink."

"Drink? What are you talking about? You don't *drink*. What's wrong with you?"

"I just had a few drinks, that's all." Marisa's speech was slow and slurred as her eyes began to close.

"Marisa? Marisa? What the hell? Marisa!"

"Huh?" She opened her eyes.

"What do you mean? You've been drinking?"

"Tiffany, I'm grown! If I want to drink that's my business. You're not my mom. Firstly, you're not passive like my mom. Secondly, you're like, well, you're black. So you can't be my—" Marisa's brows furrowed in confusion. "Well, maybe you could. But you're not—"

"Girl," Tiffany took a deep breath. "Marisa, what's going on? This isn't like you."

"He took my shoe," she whimpered. "He took my shoe. Now, I don't have a match."

"Your shoe? Who took your shoe? Oh goodness, Marisa, I'm going to call Ryan and ask him to go by there and check on you."

"Can Ryan get my shoe?"

"No," Tiffany took a nervous deep breath. "Marisa, Marisa…"

"I'm going back to sleep now. Talk to you tomorrow."

"Marisa!"

But she had already dropped the phone on the bed without hanging up. Tiffany could hear her heavy breathing on the other end. Unable to awaken her, Tiffany hung up. She thought for a moment then sighed a sense of relief knowing that her girl was safely at home.

The next morning Marisa was awakened by the doorbell. Sitting up quickly, she grabbed her head. The room appeared to be spinning. Still clothed she made her way to the front door. "Who's there?" she said as she looked through the peephole.

"It's Ryan. Sorry to drop in so early. Tiff called me and was worried about you. I told her I would stop by on my way to the office. So what's up? She said you had some kind of night last night."

"Oh yeah. I, um, I went to the little tavern down the street. You know girl's night out." Marisa tried to laugh but her head was pounding.

"So do you have any lemons in the kitchen?"

"Yeah I think so, why?" Marisa could barely open her eyes. She rubbed her temples waiting for his answer.

"Well, lemon water is good for a hangover."

"I think my bed is more of what I need right now. My head is pounding."

"Is there anything I can do before I go?" Ryan stood up from the chair he had sat in.

"No, I think I'll be fine."

"Okay, well, I'm out. Got some clients I've got to pick up."

She walked Ryan to the door. Shielding her eyes from the light she waved to him as he got in his car and drove down the street.

Marisa managed to get back to her bedroom. She sat on the side of the bed still rubbing her temples. Glancing over at the brochures she had read the day before, she thought about the decision she was about to make.

I have no choice. I can't have this, this...I will call tomorrow to schedule a counseling session. Yeah, tomorrow.

She went to the kitchen, pulling lemon juice from the fridge, then filled a glass with water. "Lemon juice and water? Well, here goes."

Marisa held the glass up as if to toast the air. "Bottoms up," she said as she drank the water and made her way back to her bedroom.

Just as she was pulling the covers over her head her cell rang. "Hello?"

"Hi, Marisa?"

"Mom? Hi. Um, what a surprise."

"I'm just calling to see how you're faring, honey. I tried calling last night but I didn't get an answer. Is everything okay?"

"Um, yeah, Mom, I um, I went out last night and totally forgot my phone. I'm doing good, though. My place is coming together and work is great."

"Well, that's good, sweetheart. Is Tiffany there?"

"No. She was here but she had to go back to the states."

"Ohhhh, so you're there alone? I thought Tiffany was staying."

"Well, she was, Mom. She just had to handle some things. She'll be back."

"Oh, okay. I worry, you know."

"I know, but I'm okay."

"Your father says hello and he misses you."

Marisa paused for a second. "Tell him hello. Um, Mom, I gotta go, okay? Will talk again soon."

"Oh, okay, honey. Take care of yourself."

"I will. Bye, Mom."

Marisa hung up the phone. Sitting there for a moment she thought of her father. She wondered if things would have turned out differently if he had been at her graduation. They were supposed to have dinner that night. Slowly, she pulled the covers back over her head.

The next morning Marisa was up early to catch her bus. The little town had already awakened as people walked the sidewalks and cars travelled up and down the cobblestone streets.

The bus pulled up to the stop, but she had to run a few feet to reach it. She had been catching the connecting bus to get to 23 Bank street for three weeks now. As she boarded she saw Samantha. Her head was buried in a newspaper.

"Hey, Sam."

Sam looked up. "Hey, girl. Ready for another week?"

"Humph, not really."

"Honey, you just started. You can't be getting tired already."

"No, just a lot going on."

Detecting the stress in Marisa's voice, Samantha turned towards her. "Look, I don't mean to pry into your business, nor am I trying, but I'm here if you need a listening ear. I'm a pretty good listener, ya know." Sam nudged Marisa's shoulder with hers as she smiled.

"Thanks, Sam. I," Marisa thought for a second as she contemplated accepting her invitation. "Thanks, maybe, well…it's nothing, really. I just have some things I need to take care of, that's all."

"Sure thing, kiddo. I understand."

They sat quietly the rest of the way to Bank Street.

"Next stop 23 Bank Street," the driver's voice echoed over the intercom.

Marisa stared up at the scrolling marquee.

"Well, here we are." Sam folded her newspaper in half. "Marisa?"

"Oh sorry, Sam."

Marisa stood up and headed for the door. They ran across the street and made a beeline for their favorite coffee shop. As they walked in the little bell above the door jingled.

"I hate that thing. Why would you want to listen to that all day?"

Marisa shrugged her shoulders.

"Honey, come on. You know a girl's gotta have her latte before work." Sam walked up to the counter. "Double expresso white chocolate mocha, please. What are you getting today, Marisa? The same?"

"Yeah, the same."

"She wants a, um, black coffee." Sam dropped her head and sighed in mock dismay.

"Stop, Sam." The girls giggled as Marisa gently shoved her in the back.

"I don't know how anyone can drink plain old black coffee. That's like—like drinking ashes with a shot of nasty."

"Well, I like a little nasty with my coffee."

They found a table by the door.

"Ooo, this is a good spot. If someone comes in looking weird, we have quick access to the outside."

"Why would you think like that, Sam?"

"Did I ever tell you the story about the robbery?"

"No!" Marisa took a sip of coffee.

"When I was in college I worked at this retail shop. One evening as we were getting ready to close up a couple of guys came in. Of course we thought they were just regular customers, so I paid them no mind. We take in our shipments through the entrance door and the back door. So I wasn't near either one when the guys pulled out hand guns. I think I peed my pants that day…"

Marisa looked shocked as she continued listening to Sam's story.

"There was one girl that was near the door. She took off like a flea hopping from Raid, girl. I, on the other hand, was stuck, right in the middle of the floor at the dress rack."

"Did they take the money? Did anyone get hurt? Like, did they catch them?"

"Luckily, no one was hurt, but they did get a few dollars. Not much because we didn't have a key to the drop vault, just a little cash in the drawers. Needless to say, I quit that night so whatever happened from there I don't know. I vowed that if I can't be near a door or not have my back turned to it, I'm not sitting."

Marisa shook her head in disgust. "It's a shame that people can be so bold as to violate another person that way. They don't care that their actions can ruin a person's life. All they're thinking about is themselves."

Sam listened attentively as she spoke. "I get the feeling you have your own story to tell."

Marisa looked at her. She felt a bit embarrassed and wondered if she had been that transparent for Sam to discern that she was speaking of herself. She took a sip of her now lukewarm coffee.

"Um, no. I mean, I know there are people out there like that."

"Mmm-hmmm." Sam took another sip of her coffee. She looked at her watch. "Geez Louise! It's seven fifty! Girl, we'd better get going."

Marisa looked at her watch. "Yeah, guess you'd better."

Sam looked puzzled as she grabbed her purse and newspaper.

Marisa only smiled as she looked at the bewildered expression that had begun to show on Sam's face.

"No worries. I'm going to come in around nine for a meeting, then I'm out."

"Wow, must be nice."

"Actually, I worked so many hours last week on the Clemson deal—a deal we snagged by the way." Marisa smiled.

"You go, girl. That's awesome!" Sam gave her a high-five. "You make me proud."

"Thank you," she said as she curtsied twice.

"Well, I gotta run. Talk soon and congrats again!"

Sam hurried out the door and down the street, while Marisa sat back down at the table. She grabbed her laptop from the bag she was carrying to go over her notes for the meeting. Just then the bell on the door jingled again.

Instinctively, she looked up. Sam's story about the robbery was still fresh in her mind. And what she saw made a chill race up her spine.

They had not seen her as they walked up to the counter, so Marisa slowly placed her laptop back into the bag. Since their backs were still turned, she had the chance to run out the door. Her heart racing inside her chest, her adrenaline pumping wildly, Marisa's anger increased the more she thought about what she had just seen. She made her way to the office building where she sat in the lobby, confused and annoyed. She shook her head in disbelief.

Ryan! And who the hell was that he was with? Couldn't have been a client—not kissing her on the cheek like that. That no good son of a—

"Hi, Marisa."

Marisa looked up. One of the girls that worked with her on the Clemson account was standing above her.

"Oh, hi. I was just sitting here killing time before the meeting."

"Well, it's about that time. See you there."

The woman walked down the corridor and disappeared into an elevator. Marisa took a deep breath as she placed her hand on her forehead. Glancing at her watch, she had three minutes to get to the meeting.

Slowly she stood up from the chair, her heart still racing inside her chest. *This is going to break Tiff's heart.* Marisa walked down the corridor to the elevator. The thought of Ryan and that *woman* in the coffee shop weighed heavily on her mind.

Marisa gave her presentation to the board members. Her success had made her the top associate in her department.

"Well, young lady, you certainly are holding your own."

"Thank you, Mr. Kubrick."

"Yes, I see a promising future for you here. Keep up the great work."

"Thank you. I will."

Marisa smiled and shook other board members' hands as she headed out the room. She found herself standing in front of one of the bathroom mirrors. For a long moment she stared at her reflection as she touched her abdomen.

How did my life come to this?

Looking down at her watch, she then pulled a pamphlet from her purse and headed out the door.

"Hi, I'm here to see Dr. Corning."

The receptionist checked her computer's list of appointments and schedules.

"Oh, yes, Miss Webb. You can have a seat. Dr Corning will be with you shortly."

Marisa sat in a corner chair in the waiting room. A black landline phone sat on an end table nestled between her chair and a grey couch on the opposite side.

What a dinosaur, Marisa thought. *Who even uses these things anymore?*

Just then a woman came and sat near it. She removed a small piece of paper from her purse and grabbed the phone from the table to make a call.

Oh! Well, I guess that just answered my question.

"Miss Webb?" A voice said as a door opened near the waiting room.

Marisa stood and followed the woman to a large weighing machine. After taking her weight and vitals, she was led to an examining room.

"Dr. Corning will be in shortly." The woman smiled as she closed the door behind her.

Here I am again. Dang, this looks like the same room I was in the last time.

There was a soft knock at the door as it opened.

"Hello, again, Miss Webb."

"Hello, Dr. Corning. You can call me Marisa."

Dr. Corning smiled. "Okay, Marisa. Did you have the opportunity to look over the materials I gave you?"

"Yes, I—I did."

"Okay, so have you throughly thought about the pregnancy and what you want to do about it?"

Marisa could hear the empathy in Dr. Corning's voice. "I have and—and I've decided to terminate this pregnancy."

"Are you sure?"

She hesitated. "Yes, I'm sure. I can't have this…"

Dr. Corning touched her hand. "It's okay. I just want to make sure you are making this decision on your own and that you're absolutely sure."

Marisa nodded her head in agreement with Dr. Corning.

"Okay, then. I will set up the appointment for you. Here's the address and physician's name. Please call me if you have any questions, or if you change your mind, honey."

Marisa took the card from the doctor's hand and walked out of the office some time later. She sat on the bench across the street, the same place she had sat just days earlier. Staring at the card in her hand, Marisa felt a wave of anxiety.

This is the only way. If I didn't do this everyday would be a reminder of the rape. Everyday, I would remember that night. I would feel the rage, the anger, and the hate as it flooded my core. No one should ever have to live like that.

The bus pulled up and the door swung open. Marisa was still in deep thought, still staring at the card. The driver, recognizing Marisa as a frequent rider, called out to see if she was still going to board. She looked up and slowly shook her head *no*. The door began to close.

"Wait! Is there a bus that goes to Finchley from here?"

"Finchley? Uh, yes it does, but it goes in the opposite direction in about an hour. You may want to cross the street over there, miss."

Marisa looked to the other side of the street. "Oh, okay. Thank you."

The driver closed the door and continued down the street. Grey smoke billowed from the back of the bus and disappeared into the sky. She looked at her watch. Just as she crossed the street, a taxi cab drove by. Marisa hailed it and jumped in.

"I need to go to this address in Finchley, please."

The driver took the card.

"How long is the drive?"

"About forty minutes, or less, ma'am."

"Oh, okay. Thank you."

Preparing for the long drive, Marisa sat back. Thoughts flooded her mind. She felt in her heart she was doing the right thing. She wondered what Tiffany would think...or if she would ever tell her. Her best friend had always been against abortions. And there was no *way* she could ever tell her parents. This was something she felt she would have to face alone.

What was only supposed to be a thirty-minute drive felt more like hours. The cab finally pulled up to a red brick building. Several people adorned the sidewalk in front with anti-abortion signs, picketing.

Feeling a bit intimidated, Marisa hesitated to get out of the car. She looked up at the building. A sign on the door read *Planned Parenthood*. Steps with black rails on either side lead up to a light brown door. A small tinted vertical window ran from the top of the door to the bottom.

She finally got out of the cab and made her way inside the building. The waiting area was small. A couple sat at one end of the room; the woman was visibly upset as the man held her hand. Another woman sat quietly as she held a magazine in her hand, her head leaning back against the wall. A voice box was housed inside the window when she made it to the counter. An opening large enough for a clipboard was just below it.

Stepping up to the glass window, she said, "Um, hi. My name is Marisa Webb. I have a three-fifteen appointment."

"Hello, Miss Webb. Were you referred by a physician?"

"Yes. Dr. Corning."

"Okay. One moment." The office assistant typed something onto the computer. The printer emitted four pieces of paper. "Here you go. We have your information, it was sent to us by Dr. Corning's office. I just need you to read over and sign these four documents, please."

Marisa took the papers that the assistant pushed through the opening. After signing them she was called to the back. A gown was handed to her, and she changed.

I'm about to do this. Marisa shut her eyes tightly and took a deep breath.

"Hello, Miss Webb?"

Marisa opened her eyes to see a woman about her mid-forties standing near her in scrubs.

"Yes?"

"I'm Dr. Margaret Taylor. How are you?"

"Well, I'm good, I guess...under the circumstances."

"I understand. Let me try to ease your mind as much as I can. I know this is not an easy thing for most women to do. Some, after the process, do have to have counseling. And some don't. Some know it's the best decision for them and are relieved afterwards. Each person is different."

Marisa simply nodded her head as Dr. Taylor went over the procedure with her.

"Lastly, Miss Webb, have you had anything to eat, drink or chew in the last four hours?"

Marisa shook her head.

"Have you had anything to smoke in the last four hours?"

"Um, no. I—I don't smoke."

Dr. Taylor looked up and smiled at Marisa as she completed the form in her hands. "Okay, well you're all set. You'll be fine."

"Thank you, Dr. Taylor." Marisa was slightly sedated and wheeled down a short corridor to a separate room as everything around her became a blur.

The next morning Marisa awakened to the stillness of the day. She stared at the ceiling, and placed her hand on her belly. A tear rolled down her cheek, but she quickly rubbed it away. She took a deep breath, still listening to the softness of the early morning sounds. The only other sound that could be heard was the gentleness of her breathing.

A faint ring gradually grew louder. Marisa turned to look at her phone. She could see who it was, and simply stared at it as Tiffany's name rolled across the screen. After the fifth ring the sound stopped. Marisa turned her face back towards the ceiling.

I know I did the right thing. Who in their right mind would want to constantly be reminded that they were violated? That their right to say yes or no was violently taken away from them? That their soul was ripped away from them by a selfish, cruel and thoughtless individual who didn't care that he were ruining another person's life just to satisfy their sick fantasy...?

She took another deep breathe as she slowly turned to her side. Feeling the discomfort she bit her bottom lip against the pain. A prescription she had filled sat on the nightstand. She grabbed the bottle of pain pills and reached for the glass of water she had placed there as well.

She glared at the prescription for a moment, reading the words: *Take two as needed for pain.* Squeezing the bottle in her hand she tightly closed her eyes. She felt the rage that had begun to rise up inside of her. Tears found their way down her cheeks as she shook two pills into her palm. For a second she just stared at the two white pills while holding the water in the other hand. She quickly took the pills and laid back on the pillow. Just then her phone rang again, and she grabbed it.

"Hello?"

"Hi, Rissa, how's it going?"

"Good, Tiff."

"I tried calling you earlier. I figured you were in the shower, or something, getting ready for work."

"Um, no I'm not going in the rest of the week."

"What? Are you sure you're okay?"

"Yes. I wish you'd stop asking me that."

"Well, I—I wasn't trying to agitate you. I mean, I was just…"

"I know, Tiff. I'm sorry. I'm just not feeling like myself today, that's all. I didn't mean to snap at you."

"It's okay. I should be there in another couple of weeks. I'm so excited!"

"Yeah, me too. So have you heard from Ryan?"

"Actually, I haven't spoken with him in a couple of days. I've been pretty busy and I guess he has been, too."

"I'm sure he *has*…"

Tiffany detected a bit of sarcasm in Marisa's voice. "Why did you say it like that?"

"Like what?"

"Like, well, something's wrong?"

"No, I was just wondering if you had talked to him, that's all."

An awkward silence expanded between them for a moment before Marisa started feeling uncomfortable. "You there, Tiff?"

"Um, yeah. Oh, guess who I saw the other day?"

"Who?"

"Matt."

Marisa felt a cold chill at the mention of his name. "He's back in the states?"

"Yeah. He said—"

"Wait, you *spoke* with him?"

"Yes. He said he was in the states for a few days but was headed back to London soon. He has a job there."

"What?" Marisa cautiously sat up on the side of the bed. "What do you mean he has a job here? Where?"

"He said on, ummm, oh! 23 Bank Street."

"So that *was* him I saw…"

"What? Who did you see?"

"Remember, I—I was standing at the bus stop with a co-worker when I looked across the street. There was a guy standing against the street light. I tried to look closer but the bus was pulling up. By the time I looked again, apparently, he had boarded the other bus going in the opposite direction."

"Well, maybe you'll run into him, huh? Wait, do you still think he's..."

"I don't know, Tiff. He was there. He followed me obviously to the dorm," she sighed. "The guy wore a woodsy-type cologne. I remembered that night when he appeared out of nowhere, that faint cologne smell. It was the same fragrance of the person who attacked me."

"Are you sure, Marisa? That was very traumatic for you."

"I'm sure of this, he had on that cologne. He followed me, and the person in my room that night wore the same cologne. That's no coincidence."

"He seemed so nice, Marisa."

"Yeah, I'm sure a lot of rapists are nice, until they violate you. So, did he say exactly when he was coming back this way?"

"He said in a few days. I don't know I'm thinking maybe a week or so."

"What else did he say?"

"Well, he *did* tell me about the airport and the way you hightailed it to the boarding entrance. Oh, and he said he thought he had seen you on twenty-third, but he wasn't sure."

For a moment Marisa sat silently then she became enraged the more she thought of Matt being in London. "Oh, okay, Tiff. I gotta go."

"Wait! Where are you going? I thought you were off the rest of the week..."

"I am but I have a few things I need to do."

"Oh, okay. I, um, guess I'll talk to you again soon. Love you, girl."

"Love you too, Tiff."

Marisa made her way to the bathroom and took a shower. She slowly dressed and headed out the door. Just as she stepped out of the apartment some people were exiting a cab near the bus stop. She hailed him, thankful that he had spotted her and backed up to where she was standing. "Camden Town, please."

"Sure thing, ma'am." The cab slowly pulled onto the cobblestone road and made it's way to her destination.

7
A Volatile Turn

Marisa settled herself in for the ride to Camden Town, grabbed her cell phone and began scrolling through the Internet.

Guns, guns. Let's see. Gratestone Guns, Forty forty-two Camden Street. Okay, I'll check this one out.

Marisa sat back in the seat. Staring out the window, her mind wandered back to the conversation she just had with Tiffany. The thought of Matt being that close made her shiver. The incident was still so fresh in her mind like it had just happened only a few days ago. She could almost smell the woodsy cologne, remembering how it had filled her nostrils as she fought the muscular dark figure with all her strength. Suddenly, Matt's voice rang out in the distance. Startled, Marisa looked up at the cab driver.

"I said your destination, miss..." The driver looked confused as he glared at Marisa while she looked out of the window, lost in her thoughts.

"Yes, yes, thank you," she said, and paid the driver.

When she stepped out onto the sidewalk, she noticed the markets were in full operation, tourists and merchants were interacting on the sidewalks and inside stores.

Marisa looked down at the address on her phone, the gun shop was somewhere nearby. Looking around, she realized the shop was only a couple of blocks in the opposite direction from where she was facing. So, she made her way down the sidewalk. The discomfort she felt in her abdomen made the walk more challenging, and maneuvering her way through the crowds was awful.

Arriving at the gun shop, she stared at the small silver and brown gun symbol painted in between the company's name. Nervously, she walked into the store. A tall rugged man with a full salt and pepper beard and grayed side burns stepped out from a windowed office.

"Well, hello there. Name's Greyson." The man reached out to shake Marisa's hand. "Looking for anything in particular?"

"Um, yes, I'm looking for a..." she hesitated. "I'm looking for a gun, please."

The man smiled. "Let me guess. You never handled a gun, have ya now?"

Marisa blushed as she raised her head up towards the shop owner. "No. No, sir...can't say that I have."

"Well, missy, the first thing you want to do is learn how to use one. It's not hard at all. It's a long process for the license though. There's some papers you'll need to fill out and some information we would have to clear before we can give you what you need to own a gun."

With her mind still reeling with thoughts of the rape, and the sensation of a beating heart in her throat, Marisa managed to nod at the gentleman in total agreement.

"Be right back."

The man walked back inside the office. Marisa watched him open a filing cabinet and pull out some papers. The shop was adorned with posters and an array of pictures with smiling people holding guns and certificates. A locked counter that lined both walls was attached to the main counter, encasing an array of styles and sizes of guns. Her eyes landed on a small pink .22 caliber pistol. Her hands suddenly had a mind of their own, first they were hanging loosely against her body, then somehow they ended up on the gun display.

"Here you are. Everything you need to get started is in this little packet." He watched her closely as she took the papers. "I see you were eyeing the little pistol there. Would you like to check it out? It's a beaut."

"Um, no. I will take the papers to fill out and bring back. I will, um, I'll look at it then."

"Okay, young lady. We do have a class that's coming up in a few days. Get those papers back to me so we can get you certified and on your way."

"Yes sir. I will."

Marisa hurried outside. Her nerves getting the best of her, she started to feel nauseous. *Okay girl, get it together. Breathe.* She took a deep breath. The thought of having a gun and possibly taking someone's life was paralyzing. Pushing the thoughts aside, she tried hailing a cab, looking forward to ending this day and heading home.

Soon a white car pulled up to the curb. Marisa stepped back from the edge.

"Hey, want a ride?"

It was Ryan. He had recognized her as he passed on the opposite side of the street, and had turned around.

"Um, no, I'm fine. I'll catch a cab."

Ryan noticed that Marisa seemed angry and aloof. "Okay, are you sure? I'm going your way. It may be a while for a cab since its so busy down here today. Come on, I'll be glad to take you home."

Marisa looked both ways, hoping she would spot a cab. Dark clouds were gathering and she did feel a few rain drops on her face. Ryan jumped out of the car to open the door when he noticed Marisa slowly moved towards it. As soon as she was inside, the rain came down in torrents.

"Looks like I was just in time, huh?" he chuckled.

Marisa sat quietly looking out the window. All she could think about was seeing Ryan and that woman at the coffee shop.

"Sooooo, you heard from Tiffany?" he said.

"Yes, spoke with her today."

"How is she?"

"You don't know? She is your girl, right? Or have you been too busy with someone else to call her?"

"Huh?" Ryan glanced over at her for a brief second. "What is that supposed to mean?"

"Nothing, nothing at all."

For a moment they sat quietly. All that could be heard was the sound of the rain as it hit the car and the splatter of water as the tires sped through the puddles.

"So, how's things been? Vacationing early, huh?"

"No, I just had some things I had to do today."

Ryan could sense Marisa's attitude was different from the time they first met, but still tried making conversation.

"Oh, okay, ummm, guess you'll be glad when Tiffany gets back, eh?"

"Maybe...I guess."

"What do you mean *you guess*? I thought you were excited about your BFF coming back to London. Changed your mind?" Ryan smiled jokingly.

"Nothing's changed." Her face clearly showed her agitation. Very soon the car pulled up to the apartment.

"What's wrong with you, Marisa? Have I done anything? I mean like...what's up?"

"What's up? Nothing's up, but I will say this..."

Ryan looked with curiosity to hear what she had to say. "Say what?"

"If you hurt my girl, trust me, you will answer to me."

"What?! Hurt her?! What are you getting at?"

"You men think you can just do whatever you want when you want and it's okay. That we're supposed to just be okay with your selfish entitled ways when it's clear you don't give a damn about who you hurt as long as you get what you want. Well, the buck stops here! Hurt my girl and I'm going to take that real personal!"

Marisa got out of the car and slammed the door. She slowly made her way up the steps and into the apartment. Ryan sat there for a moment, wondering what had just happened. He thought of getting out and confronting her, instead he started the car. Confused, he took one last look at the little hobbit door, put the car in gear and drove away.

Marisa was still angry the next morning. She lay staring at the papers she had gotten from the gun shop. The more she thought about her situation, the angrier she became. Raising from the bed she grabbed the papers from the night stand and began filling them out.

Her cell phone rang just as she was finishing up the last section of the form. "Hello?"

"Hi girl, what 'cha doin'?"

"Hi, Tiff!" Marisa was excited to hear her voice on the other end.

"So, you still playing hooky from work, huh?"

"Um, I, like, took the rest of the week off. We've been doing so well...my boss even encouraged me to take a few days..."

"Wow, girl, you're doing great, huh?"

"Yeah. You know, I'm doin' a little sum-sum." They both laughed. "I miss you, Tiff. I um, I was in Camden the other day and ran into Ryan."

"Oh, really? That's my boo."

Marisa cringed as she thought of the coffee shop and what she had seen. "Like, Tiff, for real, you think he's a good guy?"

"Yeah, I know he's a good guy. I think I'm a pretty good judge of character. Why would you ask that question? You never seemed to *not* like Ryan before. What's happened?"

Hesitating for a moment, Marisa pondered telling Tiffany what she had seen. "Well, I was just thinking, you know, the long distance thing. Those kinds of relationships normally don't work."

"But I'm coming back. I mean, well, that's one of the reasons why I'm calling."

"What? What's going on?"

"It may be a few more weeks before I can get back."

"What do you mean? What's happened, Tiff?"

"I hit a few financial snags but everything is working out. I may have to wait for a few more weeks, that's all."

"A few more? Like how many?"

"Not sure, Marisa. Two…three. Maybe another month," she whispered under her breath.

"I heard you. Another month?!"

"It may not be that long, girl. I'm just kinda guessing."

There was an awkward moment of silence. "Sooo, have you seen Patrick?"

"I haven't, not since the other night at the bar."

"At the bar?"

"Yeah, remember when I told you I saw him at the little tavern down the street?"

"No, you didn't. So what happened?"

"Well, he claimed he was there with some friends. Supposedly, this girl and her boyfriend were outside having some lover's quarrel so he was just waiting on them to finish."

"Mm-hmmm. He's such a liar."

"Why you say that, Tiff?"

"Girl, I can smell that lie all the way over here in the U.S."

"He wasn't lying. I mean, like, why would he?"

"Girl, because he's a playa. He doesn't want you thinking he's banging anyone else because that would hurt his chances with you. That's a gamer move. Haven't I taught you anything?"

Marisa's thoughts immediately flashed back to the coffee shop. "Well, I guess he wouldn't be the only one playing games?"

"What does that supposed to mean?"

"Oh, I don't know, maybe you should ask Ryan. When was the last time you spoke with him?"

"Marisa, you got something you need to tell me because you've been saying some weird stuff. Like, what's up?"

"Nothing."

"Then why did you say that? Why did you say to ask Ryan? Oh, and the last time I spoke with him was a few days ago. I've been very busy and haven't had time to really talk to him."

Marisa wondered if she should say anything. "Well, I was just going by what you said about Patrick. Wouldn't that apply to all men. I mean, isn't that indicative of their sorry-ass nature to do what they want and take what they want either by force or under false pretenses?"

"Not really. Not all men, Marisa. Some are really good guys."

"Yeah, just like Matt?"

"What? Matt? What has he got to do with anything?"

"Nothing, Tiffany." Marisa tried to calm her emotions. "I just have a lot on my mind. I need to get off the phone so I can get myself together. I've got to go into Camden to drop off some papers."

"Oh, okay. Well, I will call you later. Oh! Wait! Rissa, are you there?"

"Yes, still here. What is it?"

"I hate to bring this up but I thought it was important."

"Okay, what is it, Tiff?"

"It was reported that a couple of days ago a female student was attacked on campus."

Marisa froze.

"She wasn't hurt. She managed to get away."

"Wait! What?!"

"Yeah, I—I just thought you should know, sweetie."

Marisa placed her hand on her forehead and tried to rub the tension out of it. The thought that someone else was attacked chilled her to the bone. "Was she able to identify the person? Like, did they say if—"

"No, Rissa. She didn't get a good look at him. It was dark. The only thing she could tell them was that he was possibly about six feet or so."

Sighing, Tiffany's voice seemed far away as she thought about that night again.

"Oh, she also said that his cologne was very distinctive."

"Huh? What was that?"

"She said she remembered that the cologne he wore smelled *woodsy*."

Marisa couldn't believe what she had just heard. It sounded like the description of her own attacker. "Tiffany, didn't you say you ran into Matt?"

"Yeah. Why?"

"You don't think that was just some coincidence, do you?"

"Look, I'm not trying to be mean or insensitive but I just think Matt is one of the good guys."

"Oh, I'm sorry, Tiffany, but he doesn't get a pass from me that easily. You weren't there! You weren't raped...I was! No man gets a pass. Not from me, not anymore. We are supposed to hold some kind of wholesome standard as women and when we do we *still* get violated only to have other fools say it was *our* fault. We—we somehow *asked* for it? I don't think so! I had on my graduation gown that night, Tiff! My graduation gown. That was supposed to be the happiest time in my life. Then some woodsy-smelling jerk comes into my dorm, forces himself on me and leaves me with this little monster inside of my body!" Marisa began to cry as a chilling silence came from the other end.

"What did you say? Marisa, what did you just say?!"

In the midst of her tirade, she had let the secret of the pregnancy slip. "I—I have to go, Tiffany."

"No, Marisa. Are you pregnant?"

She could hear Tiffany's voice tremble as her question echoed across the phone. "No, not anymore."

"Marisa, Jesus! I can't right now...why didn't you tell me?"

"I was too ashamed."

"I'm your best friend, Rissa. How could you not tell me?"

"I'm sorry, Tiffany. It all happened so quickly, I didn't have time—" Suddenly the phone went dead. "Tiffany? Tiffany!" Marisa listened for an answer. "Tiff?"

Sighing, she slowly pulled the phone from her ear, her hand falling to her lap. She laid back and stared at the ceiling. Sensing that Tiffany was hurt Marisa felt guilty for not being honest with someone who had been there for her during the darkest time in her life.

"I'm sorry, Tiff. I'm so sorry," she whispered as she closed her eyes.

Marisa stood on the opposite side of the street from the gun shop. She had managed to pull herself together and make her way to Camden. Looking at the papers in her hand, she crossed the street and went into the store.

The owner was helping another customer, so she walked over to the display to look at the same .22 caliber pistol she had noticed the other day. The anxiety she felt the last time she was in that store was no longer there. The thought of someone else being attacked had emboldened her.

"Hello, can I help you?"

Marisa turned towards the man speaking to her.

"Oh, hello. You decided to come on back, did you?" The man had remembered her from the previous day.

"Yes…yes sir. I brought back the papers," she said, handing them over.

"Okay, if you'll step over here. Oh, may I have your ID, please?" He waited patiently for her to pull out her passport. "Thank you."

"So, you said something about a class…?"

"Yes, actually you're just in time. We have a class that's starting next week from six to eight this evening. I can sign you up right now."

"Sure, I'd like to come. Thank you."

Marisa finished up all the paperwork and purchased her gun of choice. She wouldn't be able to leave with it until she had gone through the class and was cleared by law enforcement.

"Well, see you next week, Mr Greyson."

"Sure thing, Marisa. You have a great day."

Marisa made her way back across the street. Sitting on the bench at the bus stop, she glanced down at her watch. It was still early. She started walking towards a pond and spotted several grey-colored benches situated around the water. Some people sat feeding the ducks. Others strolled along the sidewalks talking and laughing.

She found a bench nestled under a weeping willow tree. The wind gently passed through its branches while she lazily watched the ducks play in the pond. They appeared to be swimming in a synchronized fashion. She watched as one by one they dove under the water and popped back up, almost in unison.

I need to call Tiff. Dang. I know I should have told her, but I just couldn't...

Marisa was in deep thought when she suddenly felt a presence. Turning around, she saw Patrick standing there.

"So, what are you doing not at work? Playing hooky?"

She smiled. "No, just took a couple of days off."

"May I sit?"

"Oh, sure, of course." Sheepishly, she stared at the ducks.

"I was, uhh, coming up the street when I saw you coming out of the gun shop up there. What, you buying...a gun?"

"Um, well, I had been looking at some."

Patrick chuckled. "Do you even know how to fire a gun? You certainly didn't seem like a wild, wild west type in college."

She smiled again. "No? Well, you just never know what you can do given the right circumstances."

He looked out towards the pond. Bending down to pick up a twig from the ground, he tossed it over into the water. "Yeah, I guess you're right about that."

There was an awkward moment of silence between them. Marisa clasped her hands together as she watched a crowd of ducks diving and emerging again from the water.

"So..." Patrick began, throwing another twig into the pond. "This Saturday night I'm going to be hanging out at the club where I saw you the other week. Wanna come?"

Marisa was hesitant to accept. "I'm not sure. I, um, I may be busy," she said, even though she knew she had no plans for Saturday. She wished Tiffany was there. While she felt she knew Patrick, she still hesitated. At least having the security of her friend around would make her more comfortable.

Patrick put his hand on Marisa's shoulder. "It's okay. Just let me know. Here...here is my phone number," he said, handing her his social card.

"Oh, okay, player. Social card, eh? Black background, gold embossed raised name. Impressive."

He smiled, and stood up, propping his right foot on the bench. Resting his arms on his leg, he leaned in. "Well, thank you. You know I'm just that kind of guy." Patrick pointed his thumb back at himself.

"Still cocky, I see." She looked up at him. The sun was setting behind him slightly obscuring her view of his face.

"Well, you know me. 'Course, I don't call it cocky. I call it confidence."

"Humph, well I call it cocky."

Patrick smiled. "I gotta run. See you Saturday night?"

"I don't know, I—"

"Be there or be square," he said as he trotted across the grass and up the small hillside.

Marisa watched as he disappeared out of sight. Smiling to herself she looked at the black and gold embossed card. *Patrick Weston.* She tapped the card with her finger, then placed it inside her pocket. A duck had perched itself near the bench in front of her. "So what do you think, Mr. Duck? Should I go?"

The duck quacked.

"Well, I don't understand duck language, but I did ask the question, huh?" Marisa stared out over the pond. She sighed as she thought of the quarrel she had had with Tiffany. *I sure miss my girl.*

She grabbed her phone and dialed the number, but hung up before it had a chance to ring.

What do I say? What if she doesn't want to talk to me?

Soon she built up her nerve and dialed the number again. The phone rang as she listened nervously.

After the third ring Tiffany's voice mail was activated. "Um, hi, Tiff. Marisa. I, um...I was just sitting here at a little pond, all alone...all by myself...alone. Just me and well, Mr. Duck here. I, well, I called to say I'm sorry about the last time we spoke. I really miss you, girl." She hesitated for a moment, then took a deep breath. "Well, guess I will catch up with you later. Bye."

Marisa hung up the phone. She rolled it around in her hand as she looked up just as a couple was passing by where she was sitting. She wondered if Tiffany had simply refused to answer the phone.

She looked out over the pond, tucking her phone back inside her purse. She leaned forward towards the duck that had perched itself in front of her earlier. With his head slightly tucked between his wing the duck quacked once again.

"What was that again, Mr. Duck? You know, I've been feeling a lot like that myself lately. Like I just want to tuck my head and just—" Marisa stopped mid-sentence. She grabbed her phone from her purse and dialed another number. The phone rang.

"Hello?" A voice said on the other end.

"Hello, Sam? Hi there, this is Marisa."

"Oh, hi. How are you? Missed you at work this week."

"Thank you. How's work been?"

"Oh, pretty much the same. Everybody's still playing their roles. You know how that goes. We still don't seem to be able to get any Indians. Chiefs all over the place."

Marisa and Sam laughed.

"Hey look, I, um...I was invited out by a college acquaintance of mine. I was wondering if you'd like to go with me tomorrow night? Like, I'd just feel more comfortable if I wasn't going alone."

"Um, well, I haven't made any plans and I can't think of anything I have to do at the moment. Why, sure, of course. I'd be delighted to go with you. Give me a call tomorrow."

"Awesome! Thanks, Sam."

"No problem. Thanks for inviting me. Talk soon...smooches."

"Okay, call you tomorrow." Marisa hung up the phone and looked down at the duck. "That was a brilliant idea, Mr. Duck. Thank you," she said as she smiled down at it.

She stood up and took a deep breath, then exhaled. Panning around the pond once more, she then headed up the small hillside to the bus stop so she could finally go home.

It was Saturday morning and the little town was up and alive. Marisa awakened to the brisk aroma of coffee that filled her bedroom.

"Mmmmm, coffee..." she stretched. "Nothing like a smart coffee pot." She lay there for a minute, thinking of seeing Patrick. Grabbing her phone, she called Samantha's number.

"Hello?"

"Hi, Sam...Marisa."

"Oh, Good morning, lady. Everything okay?"

"Yes, yes. I know it's early. I was just, um, calling to see if we were still on for tonight?"

"Sure thing. I have a few errands to take care of today. Oh! We'll have to catch the three-forty coach, well, three-twenty for me."

"Alright. See you then."

Marisa hung up the phone and laid it on the night stand. *Guess I'll get up and do a few things myself.* Just then her phone rang. She became a little nervous as she watched Tiffany's name scroll across the face of the phone. She took a deep breath. "Hello?"

"Hi, Marisa...Tiffany."

"I know, um, how are you?"

"Good, good. I got your message so...I, well, I know we haven't talked in a while..."

"Yeah. I know. I just wanted to say I was sorry, Tiffany. I'm so sorry I wasn't totally honest with you. I was so in shock and ashamed. I was felling so—"

"Marisa, you don't have to explain to me. I should have been more understanding. I'm sure that whole thing was so horrible for you. I guess I was being a bit selfish."

"No, you're my best friend. I should have reached out to you. We've been friends since—elementary school," she started saying just as Tiffany finished the sentence with her.

They laughed, knowing that they had done that a million times over the course of their friendship.

"I know you would have hopped a plane and been here for me, girl. I knew you were hurt when you weren't answering my calls."

"Yeah, I guess I was being a bit petty. You know me— Petty Betty."

The girls laughed again.

"I'm glad you called. I miss you so much, Tiff. Oh! Guess what?"

"I'm listening." Tiffany was eager to hear what had the sound of tea to it.

"Well...I ran into Patrick yesterday."

"Patrick? Really?! What happened?"

"He, uh, asked me out to the Button Down Disco tonight."

"Really? So are you going?"

"At first I wasn't but then I called a co-worker to see if she wouldn't mind tagging along. We're supposed to meet up later today to head over to Camden."

"Oh, okay. Soooo, you got a new BFF, huh?"

Marisa chuckled. "Noooo. Who could replace you, girl?"

"Exactly. So what is she like? Is she cute like me? You know, all this saucy melanin and all."

"Well, she's actually quite nice. We have mostly hung out at the little coffee shop just on the next block from work. She, um, well, oh...she hipped me to some of the people I would be working with."

"How so? Like, are they not nice people or something?"

"Oh, no. It's like..." Marisa thought for a moment. "It's like not being in an unspoken, yet visibly hostile environment."

"That sounds like an environment I would get into trouble in."

"Yeah, Tiff, you probably would. You know your mouth. When it comes to keeping it real, you just say whatever."

"I sure do. That way people don't have to speculate where you're coming from because they always know where you stand."

"So, Tiff, when will you be back? I'm so lost without youuu…"

"Humph, I can't tell. You're getting ready to hang out with your new best friend, by the way…what's her name?"

"Oh, Sam. Actually, Samantha. She's really cool."

"Mm-hmm. Well, anyway. Things haven't been going quite like I'd hope but it's looking like within the next couple of months, maybe, or less."

"Wow. Oh, have you talked with Ryan?" For a minute there was silence. Long enough that Marisa looked at her phone to see if she was still connected to the call. "Tiff? Hello, Tiff?"

"I'm here."

"Oh, for a sec I thought I'd lost you."

"Umm…Ryan? Well, I kinda broke it off."

"What?!" Marisa tried to show empathy. "Yeah, I figured with the distance and all, and me not being sure when I would get back I just thought it was unfair to expect him to like, be faithful, you know?"

Marisa could hear the hurt in her voice. "Are you okay?"

"Yeah, yeah. I mean it was the right thing to do."

"Maybe you're right, Tiff." She had a flashback of Ryan with his arm around the neck of another woman at the coffee shop again while she listened to her friend talk.

"Well, I'm going to let you go. I have to get on my grind if I'm going to get back to Europe."

"Ohhhh, you gotta go?"

"Yes, I do. So, get over your dependency issues."

The girls laughed, uncontrollably.

"Love you, Tiff."

"Love you, too, honey. Be careful tonight."

"Oh, you bet, girl. Besides I will have my new BFF with me."

"I'm not worried about that. I'm irreplaceable. Bye."

"Bye, Tiff."

Marisa held the phone to her ear until she heard the other end disconnect. She sat there for a minute, smiling with relief. The air had been cleared between her and Tiffany. She sprung up from the side of her bed and headed into the kitchen. Pouring herself a cup of coffee, she sipped carefully at the hot black liquid as she stared out the window.

Suddenly, the distant ringing of her phone echoed from her bedroom. She quickly walked back to the room, grabbing the phone. "Hello?"

"Hi, Marisa...Sam."

"Oh, hi. Is everything okay?"

"Yes, of course. I just wanted to tell you I'd pick you up around eight-thirty."

"Pick me up? In what?" Marisa could hear Samantha laugh on the other end.

"Well, I didn't want to say anything because I wasn't sure if I was actually going to do it or not."

"Do what, Sam?"

"Well, I had been working on purchasing a car."

"Oh, wow! That's great!"

"Yeah, I got a call from the sales office. I actually had no problems getting it. It was just a matter of making up my mind. Anyway, I picked up the car about two hours ago."

"That's wonderful, Sam. So, you're a car owner now!"

"It appears so," she giggled. "And you will be my first passenger."

Marisa smiled. "I'm honored, and I love being chauffeured."

"Oh, really? We'll see if you're still wanting to be chauffeured after tonight." The girls laughed. "Talk soon."

Marisa grabbed her coffee from the night stand. "Yep, tonight should prove to be very interesting."

The day seemed to crawl along as Marisa's anxiety increased. Standing in her bathroom mirror, she carefully brushed loosed powder across her face to set her makeup. Thoughts rushed through her mind. She pondered her motives for agreeing to go to the *Button Down Disco*. She had seen Patrick there only a few weeks earlier, and to see him there was a bit awkward for her.

The doorbell rang just as she was probing her closet for her favorite shoes. "Just a minute!" she yelled from inside her closet. She frantically searched for the match to her other shoe when she remembered it was the one she had thrown inside a driver's car on her way home from the tavern that night.

Slightly exasperated, she quickly grabbed another pair and darted towards the ringing doorbell. Looking through the peep hole, she could only see the back of a female standing there. "Sam?!" Marisa called out, still looking through the hole. She opened the door once she saw that it was her.

"Ooo girl, I'm so sorry. I couldn't find my shoe."

"That's okay, I was just standing here admiring my purchase."

"Oh, right!" Marisa looked past Samantha to get a better glimpse of the car. "Wow, a BMW X1?! Who do you work for again?!"

Samantha laughed. "Now you understand why I had to really think about this. I've been looking at this car for a while."

"It's beautiful, girl. Congrats."

"Thank you." Sam curtsied. "Would you like to help me pay for it?"

They laughed as they headed out the door for the ride to Camden Town.

The ride started out oddly quiet. The passing cars going in the opposite direction echoed faintly inside the car as they continued their journey down the highway. Samantha took a quick look over in Marisa's direction who was somberly looking out of the passenger's window.

"Earth to Marisa…"

Samantha made an effort to get her attention. Her voice seemed to echo from a distant place. For a moment Marisa remained eerily quiet. Her eyes still transfixed outside of the car. Suddenly realizing that someone was addressing her, she turned as if startled.

"Huh? I'm sorry what did you say?"

"Where is your head space, girl? You were looking out that window like you'd been hypnotized. What were you thinking about?"

Marisa thought for a while. "I—I was thinking of my college days."

"Your college days? Oh, that's where you met the gentleman that invited you out tonight, isn't it?"

"Gentleman? More like arrogant jock."

Samantha looking a bit confused, chuckled. "Arrogant jock? How so?"

"Well, he was one of those high-profile athletes…" she gestured with quotation marks. "We were in a co-ed dorm and he lived on the same floor as me."

"How delightful. Co-ed, eh?"

Marisa smiled. "It wasn't all it was cracked up to be. I mean it had its pros and cons."

"Well, what was so *con* about living in a dorm with a bunch of hot guys?" Samantha smiled as she quickly looked at the other girl. "So what's his name again?"

"Oh, um, Patrick. His name's Patrick. I don't know maybe I'm being a bit harsh, I guess. He just, well, he was always so cocky and arrogant. Sometimes he acted like an entitled little brat. I mean he was smart and all, and he knew it. He was a little bit, no, he was a *lot* flirty."

"Is he cute?" Samantha quickly interjected her question.

Marisa hesitated. "Yes, actually he is quite handsome."

"Mmm, now we're getting somewhere. So, it sounds like to me you might be a bit attracted to this guy. We women can be pretty critical of a man when we have the hots for him."

"I don't know if i had the hots for him as much as I thought he was, I don't know, intriguing?"

Samantha thought for a while. Marisa's words struck her as odd. "Intriguing, you say? Well, did you ever go out with him while you were there?"

"No," she said as she turned her face back towards the passenger window.

"Why not?"

"I don't know. I mean, he never asked me."

"Well, if you were interested in him you should have asked *him*."

"Oh no. I'm young but I'm old school, Sam. If a man is interested in me I don't think I should have to ask him out."

"No, not all the time. Sometimes I think men are very insecure, that's why they sometimes act so cocky and arrogant. That's their way of camouflaging their insecurities. Much like a smoke screen, you know?"

"Humph, I don't know. Patrick…I don't think it's a smoke screen with him. I mean, I could be wrong. My best friend think he's a jerk, too." Marisa smiled. "Course she's not very trusting of people. She feels a person has to prove loyalty before she embraces them, you know."

"Oh, I like her already. So now your best friend, what's her name…?"

"Tiffany."

"Tiffany? Manifestation of God…"

"What?" Marisa turned towards her.

Samantha took another quick glance over at Marisa. As much as the seatbelt allowed her, she was now slightly turned towards her with a look of inquisitiveness.

"Manifestation of God. That's the meaning of her name. Is she a very spiritual person?"

"Yeah, why do you ask?"

"Just because of her name. It seems only logical that she would be."

Marisa straightened herself back in her seat. "She's been there for me through some of the most difficult times in my life. It's hard to find people like her."

"I hear you. Really good friends are hard to come by. I guess that's why I don't have very many."

"So you don't have a best friend?"

Samantha smiled.

She rapped the tip of her fingernails on the steering wheel. "I do, actually. She moved away several years ago. We are still in touch and when I get the chance to see her it's like we never missed a beat. Solid friendship, you know."

"Yes."

"So are you excited about tonight? Seeing your old college friend?"

"Well, like, I've seen him here a few times since college."

"How did he end up in London? Following you?"

Marisa could see the slight grin on Samantha's face from the approaching car lights.

"I can't quite remember. I think he ended up getting an internship here."

"He sounds like a pretty interesting—" Samantha stopped speaking. The car came quickly to a slow pace and then to a stop.

"What's wrong?"

"Oh, shoot!"

Marisa followed Sam's glaring eyes to the highway ahead. Cars were bumper to bumper as far as they could see heading towards Camden Town.

"This looks bad, really bad."

"What do you mean?"

"Last time I saw it like this I was in traffic for hours. See there..."

"What?" Marisa squinted her eyes in an effort to see what she was pointing at.

"There...those glittering lights in the distance. There's been an accident or something."

Marisa grabbed her phone and looked at the time. "Ten o'clock. Is there another way?"

"There *is*, but we are dead in the middle with no turning point or exit. Wait." Samantha opened her car door and stood outside to get a better look. Soon she sat back in the car. "Oh good. They're moving. What time did you say it was?"

"Ten o'clock."

"We may still be able to make it. The traffic seems to have started moving pretty steadily now."

Marisa gave a sigh of relief as she glared back down at the time on her phone.

"For someone who thinks this guy's a jerk, you sure seem anxious to see him."

Marisa chuckled nervously. "I don't know, Sam. It's weird that I'm so nervous about this. I'm glad you came with me. Otherwise I'd be home flipping channels on the TV, or working."

"Working?!" Samantha pressed her lips together. "Once I leave work, I try not to think about it."

"I actually like what I'm doing. It's very exciting and never a dull moment, especially with my co-workers."

Samantha laughed. "Didn't I tell you they were an interesting bunch?"

"They are indeed."

Samantha leaned back into her seat. "Oh look, we're moving a bit faster now. We should be there before long."

"Awesome." She looked out at the moving traffic. Her thoughts again wondering how the night would go as they picked up speed with only three exits to go before reaching Camden Town.

Samantha's car pulled up to the valet in front of the *Button Down Disco*. Four women quickly ran across the street and passed in front of the car and onto the sidewalk. Cars moved slowly as pedestrians continued crossing back and forth from the building to the street.

"So your guy is meeting you here tonight, huh?" Samantha's words were a bit muddled as she freshened up her makeup.

"He's not my guy, Sam. We went to college together."

"Um, okay. Semantics. Let me rephrase the question. So you're meeting your college buddy here tonight?"

"I'm sorry, Sam. I'm just a bit nervous, I guess. I mean like—"

Samantha interrupted her. "It's okay. I get it. But hey, I'm with you. I got your back."

Marisa smiled. "Thanks, Sam. You're a good friend.

The valet came around to the driver's side of the door. "Valet parking, ma'am?."

"Oh, yes."

The man ran back to the other side of the car and opened Marisa's door. Then he proceeded around to the driver's side. Samantha had already opened the door with one foot touching the ground.

"Your keys, ma'am."

Samantha gave the valet her keys and walked around to stand by Marisa. "Well, here we are."

Marisa took a deep breath. "Yeah, here we are."

They walked to the back of the line. It was moving at a snail's pace. The faint sound of music could be heard through the walls as Samantha began to pop her fingers and sway back and forth to the music.

"It's been a long time since I've been here."

"Oh, you've been here before?"

"Yeah, about a year ago...I think it's been. It's always been a pretty popular place."

The line moved up a few feet.

"I wish there was an easier and faster way to get in. I don't remember standing in line when I was here the last time."

"Oh, right, you and your best friend. How long before she comes back to London?"

"I don't quite know, but—"

Just then Marisa felt a hand on her shoulder. Startled, she turned around. It was Patrick.

"I see you made it."

"Yeah, I did."

Patrick smiled as he looked over at Samantha. "And who's this lovely young lady?"

"Oh, Patrick, this is Samantha. Sam…Patrick."

He reached out to shake her hand. "Please to meet you. Sam for short, huh?"

Samantha blushed as she shook his hand. "Right you are, sir."

Marisa watched the interaction between them. "I told you he was a flirt, Sam."

"So, you've been talking about me, huh? What did she say, Sam? Hope it's okay if I call you that."

"Sure it is. That's usually what people call me. She only said she was meeting you here and, um, that you're a nice guy."

"Well that's not so bad, I guess." Patrick looked over at Marisa. "Hey, come on, ladies. I have some people waiting for us inside."

"You mean we're just going to skip this whole line of people?" Marisa motioned at the long line at both ends of the sidewalk leading to the door.

"Of course not."

Patrick led Marisa and Sam to a side door of the club. He knocked and the door opened, revealing a tall six-foot five man with triceps that looked like they had been chiseled onto his body. His voice was deep and husky as he greeted Patrick.

"What's up, Patrick? Back again tonight?"

"Yeah, you know how it is, Bo."

Marisa turned to Sam with a look of confusion on her face. She whispered to Samantha. "Bo?" The girls giggled catching Patrick and the bouncer's attention, who for a moment had forgotten they were there.

"Hey, Bo, this is Marisa...a college friend of mine, and this beautiful young lady is her friend, Samantha."

"Welcome, ladies. Come on in."

The heavy door closed behind them. They walked down a dimly lit corridor and then up a flight of stairs to a roof top of people. A DJ booth stood between the entrance and a second door on the opposite side. A string of lights encompassed the patio. White furniture was strategically placed around the perimeter of the space and a bar was nestled on the opposite side of the DJ's booth.

"Come on, I have a couple of people for you to meet." Patrick walked over to a group sitting in a semi-secluded area of the patio. "What's up, y'all?"

Four guys and three girls turned towards him as he introduced Marisa and Samantha. They all shook hands and sat back in their seats. "Have a seat, ladies." One of the men pointed to some empty seats. Patrick stood off at a distance with a woman who did not appear to be part of the group.

"Hi, I'm Angela." A blonde woman about five-foot eleven, who was sitting next to Marisa, reached out to shake her hand as she introduced herself. "I think I remember you from a few weeks ago."

"Oh?" she tried to place the young woman's face.

"Yes, I was with Patrick that night you came with your friends to the club..."

"Oh, okay."

Marisa smiled as she nervously clasped her hands together. She looked around the rooftop. Noticing Samantha standing over at the bar she excused herself and headed there, too. She appeared to be having a casual conversation with the bartender.

"Hey!" Marisa tapped her on the shoulder. "How you just gonna leave me with a bunch of strangers?"

"Marisa, calm down. You were talking so I just walked over to get a drink."

"Well, you look like you're trying to get cozy with the bartender."

"He is kinda cute, don't you think?"

Marisa looked over at him. "Okay, he's alright, I guess."

The girls chuckled.

"Here you go, Sam," the bartender said as he handed her a drink.

"Sam? Oh, you're on a first-name basis and you just met the guy?"

"But of course..." She pulled out a small social card and handed it to her.

"Brandon Rhodes, Bartender at Large. Oh, and a contact number. My, we do move fast."

"Honey, we aren't getting any younger." Samantha sipped on her drink.

Marisa noticed Patrick walking towards them. "So, this is where the two of you disappeared to."

"Yeah, I walked over to get a drink." Sam held up her glass towards Patrick.

"You mind if I take Marisa for a sec?"

She looked at Patrick with curiosity in her eyes and then back at Samantha.

"I wanted to take you on the dance floor."

She felt a small sense of relief.

"Sure, she came to have a good time and I did too." Samantha nudged her towards Patrick.

"Great!" he grabbed Marisa's hand and headed to the crowded floor. "So, are you enjoying yourself?" He pulled her close as the soft music played in the background.

"Um, it's okay."

"No, I asked you if you were enjoying yourself."

She hesitated for a moment. "Yes, it's really nice up here. Like how you did you get connected so fast in the small amount of time you've been here?"

"I actually travelled here a lot during school breaks and stuff. I've known the owner, Chris, for years."

"Wow, who knew?"

Patrick chuckled. "So, how's work? I hear you're doing really well."

Marisa pulled her head back from Patrick's shoulder to look at his face. "How do you know that?"

"Like you said, I have connections."

"So, um, it was kinda weird seeing you at the tavern the other night."

"Yeah, well, I just needed to get out for a bit and it was in walking distance."

"Oh, okay."

"Maybe we can hang out soon. I mean, like, just you and me."

"Um, sure, I guess."

Just as the music began to wane, Marisa noticed a familiar face talking to Samantha. Her legs weakened beneath her. As the music stopped, Patrick noticed the look on her face. He followed her now macabre look in the direction of where Samantha stood. Matt had made an entrance from what seemed to be out of nowhere and was having what appeared to be a pleasant conversation with her.

"Hey, are you okay?" Patrick's voice seemed miles away. Slightly nudging her shoulder, he asked again. "Are you okay?"

For a moment Marisa stood motionless. "Yes, yes." She finally managed to say as she tried to pull herself together. She couldn't allow her emotions to put her secret in jeopardy. She took a quick glance at Patrick's watch. "Wow, it's getting late."

He looked at his watch, too. "Yeah, it's getting late but this party is just getting hot."

"Um, well, I have a lot of work to do tomorrow."

"Tomorrow's Sunday..."

"I know, and I have a presentation I have to prepare for on Monday. It will probably take most of the day."

"Then how about having a drink with me before you leave...?"

"No, I can't." Marisa continued looking over at Samantha and Matt as she gathered her things. "My girl over there looks like she's had one too many and, well, someone has to drive sober."

Confused at her sudden departure, Patrick watched as she walked over to where Matt and Samantha were standing.

"Hey, girl, where you been?" Samantha said as she saw Marisa approaching.

"Hey there, little lady. Long time no see."

Marisa nervously smiled. "Come on, Sam. It's time to go."

"Go? But the party is just getting started."

"I have work to do tomorrow and you're practically wasted."

"No I'm not. I've only had, um…" Samantha's frowned. "Oh, shoot, I don't remember."

"Exactly, come on."

"This is your friend, huh?" Matt sipped on his drink as he smiled at Marisa. "Do you need help getting her to your car?"

"No, no. We can manage, thank you."

Patrick walked over as the two girls started walking toward the exit. "Hey, you need some help?"

"I guess I can use a little help."

Patrick helped Marisa down the stairs to the valet.

"Thanks, Patrick. I can handle it from here."

"Okay, well, uh…we'll talk soon."

"Yeah, soon."

The valet brought the car around. Marisa helped Samantha get into the passenger's side, then headed home.

8

A Shattered Rose

Marisa headed down the long dark highway. Only the headlights of oncoming cars gave her a way to see the broken white lines on the road. Samantha lay quiet, reclined in the passenger's seat.

"Some support you were," she sighed as she glanced over at the girl laying motionless. "I miss Tiffany so much."

Suddenly Marisa remembered why she had left so abruptly. *Matt,* she thought. He had appeared out of nowhere. The last she remembered was that he was in the states, yet there he was laughing and talking with Samantha.

"I wonder what he was talking to you about, Samantha?" Marisa looked over at her once more.

"Actually, he was talking about you."

"Huh?" She realized even though the girl lay there quiet, Samantha had heard the question. "You're awake?"

"I've never been asleep. My head was feeling light so I just wanted to lay quiet for a moment." Samantha raised her hand and rubbed her forehead. "I haven't been out in a very long time. I was always working and just didn't have time. I guess I was making up for lost time," she sighed.

"So, you said Matt was talking about me?"

"Yeah, I think you have a secret admirer."

Marisa glared over at Samantha. "What do you mean?"

"Just that he spoke very fondly of you. He told me about the night of your graduation and how you were spooked at the dorm when you saw him. That's what we were laughing about."

Marisa felt a deep feeling of anxiety in the pit of her stomach. "Well, I didn't think it was funny. I felt like I was being stalked."

Samantha pressed the button on the side of the arm rest to raise her seat. "Well, he said he saw you walking to your dorm, that it was dark and you seemed upset so he followed you to make sure you got there safely."

Marisa glanced in the rear view mirror, then the side mirror as she passed a car in front of her. "Get there safely?" She became visibly angry at Matt's excuse for following her.

"That's what he told me. Listen, I don't know the guy but he seemed pretty nice."

"Exactly, Sam. You don't know him or what he's capable of."

Samantha was confused, becoming inquisitive about her statement. "What do you mean?"

She had said too much. "Nothing nothing. Just stay away from him." Marisa looked in the rearview mirror again. "That car behind us..."

Samantha turned to take a look. "Yes, what about it?"

"It's been behind us for the last several miles. I noticed it quickly passed around the car back there when I went around."

"So? Maybe they just can't get around you. You are driving pretty fast, you know."

"No, I picked up speed only when I noticed that car."

Samantha looked again. "Well, we're almost to our exit. Let's see what it does when we get off."

Curiously, they watched the other car as they took the exit ramp. The car behind them exited as well. "See, I told you. That car is following us, Sam"

"Maybe, maybe. Um, slow up, Marisa."

When she slowed down, the car behind them slowed down, too. They both became instantly nervous.

"Who would be following us?" Samantha looked at her with fear in her eyes.

"I don't know. Let's pull over to this gas station like we're going to get gas."

"Okay."

She pulled the car into the station and up beside a gas pump. The car slowly passed by and continued down the road.

"Maybe they weren't following us, Marisa."

"No, that car was following us. Did you recognize it?"

"No, did you?"

"No."

They looked at each other.

"Well, I'll stay at your place tonight. I don't think I should drive anyway and, well, I'm a little creeped out."

"Yeah, I wouldn't want to go home by myself right now either."

Marisa put the car in drive and slowly pulled out from the gas station. She couldn't help but think that once again Matt was following her. She wanted so desperately to tell Samantha the truth about him, but every time she attempted to, something in her heart wouldn't let her. It was too painful to think of, let alone talk about. The rest of the ride to Marisa's apartment, they watched every car with suspicion.

"And here we are," she said as they pulled up to the door.

Samantha yawned, stretching her hands above her head. Marisa opened her door when she noticed a car parked a few feet down the road. It appeared to be the same car that was following them. Without saying anything to Samantha, she quickly walked around to the other side.

"Come on." Marisa went up the stairs to unlock the door. Still feeling light-headed, Samantha slowly opened her door. "Come on, Sam."

She could sense the urgency in Marisa's voice. "Wha—what's wrong?" She looked confused as she walked up the steps toward the door.

Once inside Marisa quickly locked the door behind them. "I believe that car that was following us is parked down the road."

"What?! You've got to be joking!"

"No, I'm not joking, Sam."

She walked to her bedroom window. Samantha followed closely behind her. Just as she peeked slightly through the curtains, the mysterious car sitting in the shadows slowly moved down the street towards the tavern.

"This is a bit scary, Marisa. Who in the world would want to follow us?"

"Not us, Sam. Me."

"What?!"

Marisa watched as the car disappeared out of sight. She let the curtains fall back over the window and walked dazedly to sit on the bed.

"What do you mean, you?"

"It's a long story."

Marisa laid her purse on the bed and then clasped her hands together. Taking a deep breath she turned towards Samantha who was now sitting beside her on the bed. After a brief moment, she lifted her head.

"That night, after the graduation, I was upset. My dad had left the ceremony early. I don't even know if he stayed long enough to see me walk across the stage. We were all supposed to go out and celebrate. I was so angry I decided not to go with my mom to the restaurant. Instead, I was going to go to this after grad party at one of the Fraternity halls. I was so angry, I walked to my dorm to change clothes. It was so dark and I stood outside looking for my key when all of a sudden I hear this voice speaking to me. It was Matt. He startled me that night. That's what he was referring to...I guess he was following me."

Samantha listened intently. Marisa turned her face towards the ceiling. She focused on the fan blades as they turned slowly.

"I forgot to lock my door and was focused on getting dressed for the party. So just as I was about to step into the shower I heard something."

Marisa's eyes became clouded with tears. One slowly streamed down the side of her face saturating her dark blonde hair.

"I tip-toed to the bathroom door. I was scared and tried to get to the door quickly, but before I could shut it someone opened it with enough force to make me fall backwards. I think I hit my head on the bathtub. I'm not sure. I was dazed, Sam. I tried to fight back, but I couldn't. Whoever it was was too strong and my head...I don't know, I was dazed. I wanted to fight back but I couldn't..."

Marisa began to sob as she placed her hands over her face. Samantha, her eyes now filled with tears, couldn't believe the story she was hearing. She gently touched and clasped her hand around Marisa's.

"I'm so sorry. I'm so very sorry."

They were quiet for what seemed like hours. Marisa lay with her arm across her face. Samantha sat numbed at what she had just revealed to her.

"Are you going to be okay, honey?"

Marisa slowly raised up on both her elbows. "Yeah, I'll be fine. I'm beginning to realize that even though I feel so ashamed, I can't hide this anymore."

Samantha reached over again and softly squeezed her hand. "No. Because it's not your fault. You did nothing wrong. That scum took advantage of you, that's what he did."

She closed her eyes and took a deep breath. "I question everything I did that night. I wasn't thinking I was that angry. I walked by myself, in the dark. I should have locked the door. I—"

Samantha stopped her in mid-sentence. "Marisa, listen to me, no woman, no matter how she chooses to dress or what she does or does not do gives anyone the right to violate her, ever! Don't blame yourself for the actions of someone who was obviously sick and selfish. Wherever he is, he will get his. Karma's a—"

Marisa interrupted her. "Sam, he's here, here in London."

Samantha stopped speaking. "What?"

Marisa turned towards her. "He's already here."

"Who's here?"

"The guy who raped me."

"How do you know that?"

She paused. She didn't know if she should tell Samantha who she suspected.

"Who Marisa?"

"Matt. The guy you were talking with tonight."

"Matt. What?!" she exclaimed.

"Yes."

"No, I can't believe it. He seems so sweet." Samantha sat confused and perplexed. "That's why you said what you said...about staying away from him."

"Yes."

"Wow, I—I mean, I have no words."

Samantha leaned back on the bed post. Marisa slowly laid back down on the bed. Soon, sun rays pushed their way through the bedroom curtains and into the hallway outside the room. The two of them lay across the bed. Neither had slept a wink.

The sound of a domestic flight echoed from the outside as Marisa looked over at Samantha. Still propped up against the bed pole, her eyes were closed.

"Hey, you asleep?"

"No. I'm too wired to even think about sleep."

"I'm sorry, Sam. I didn't mean to unload all of my baggage on you."

"It's okay. If you can't confide in your friends, then who?"

"Aw, thank you, Sam...for being here for me."

"No problem, I think you'd do the same for me."

Samantha looked at her watch. "I guess I'd better get going. I have some reports I need to work on for an early Monday meeting." She started putting on her shoes. "Are you going to be okay?"

"Of course. I have some things I need to get done as well."

Marisa walked her to the door. Leaning on the outside rail, she watched as Samantha got into her car. "Take care. Will pick you up tomorrow."

"Sure thing, Sam."

Marisa waved goodbye as she watched the car drive down the cobblestone street. She looked down at the spot where she saw the strange car parked late last night, then a strange and ominous feeling sent chills up her arms. She closed the door quickly just as her cell phone rang.

Rushing to her room, she dove across the bed and grabbed the phone from the nightstand on the opposite side.

"Hello!"

"Hi, is the lady of the castle in?" The voice said on the other end.

"But of course she is." For a brief moment there was silence then joyful screaming. "Tiffany!" Marisa yelled. "Omg!! It's so good to hear your voice." Marisa turned right side up on the bed towards the ceiling fan that hummed above her.

"It's good to hear yours, too, honey. How are you? I miss you so much."

Marisa was so overwhelmed from the night that she began to cry.

"Ohhhh, why are you crying, Rissa?"

"I don't know if I'm cut out for this, Tiffany."

"What do you mean? What's happened? Is work okay?"

"Yeah, work is fine."

"Then what do you mean?"

She began telling Tiffany about the party, seeing Matt, and the suspicious car they had seen down the street.

"Marisa, you're creeping me out. So what did you do when you saw the car?"

"I came inside and locked the door."

"What did…Samantha, right?"

"Yes, that's her name."

"What did she do? Did she see the car?"

"Yes, she did. We looked out the bedroom window just as it slowly drove away."

"I'm really worried. You really need to think about what I said about getting some protection."

"I know, I know. I've been thinking about it." Marisa looked at the application for the gun permit sitting on the nightstand. Now more than ever she knew what she had to do. "I actually looked at one last week."

"You did? Well, that's a step in the right direction."

"I'm still not absolutely convinced about this gun thing, Tiffany."

"Listen, you need to protect yourself, especially if Matt's there. God forbid if he knows where you live." For a moment they didn't speak. "So, on a lighter note, guess what?"

Marisa could hear the excitement in Tiffany's voice. "What?"

"Everything's cleared up here and I should be flying back in the next few weeks."

Marisa fell back on the bed kicking her feet in the air. Tiffany could hear her excitement over the phone.

"Calm down, girl!"

"I can't. You've always been there for me, Tiff. I need your friendship now more than ever."

"Humph, I thought you found *another* bff."

Marisa and laughed. "Stop playing, Tiffany."

"I'm just kidding. Oh! And guess what else? Ryan and I spoke on last week and, well, when I get back we're going to see where it goes."

Marisa was not expecting to hear the news she had just given her. She wasn't sure if she should tell her friend about seeing him at the coffee shop.

"Hello? Marisa? Are you there?"

Her thoughts had taken her away from the conversation. "Oh, yeah. I'm here. I'm sorry. Tiffany are you sure that's what you want to do? I mean…"

Tiffany could tell that Marisa didn't seem to enthused about the idea of Ryan and her getting back together. "Marisa, what's wrong? You liked Ryan. Now you seem like, well, like you're not so gung-ho on *him and me* anymore. What's happened? What are you not telling me?"

Marisa hesitated, but a flash back of Ryan with his arm around a woman's neck and kissing her on the cheek was more than she could stand. "Tiffany, a few weeks ago I was at a small coffee shop just down from the building where I work." She stopped for a moment.

"Go on." Tiffany was anxious to hear what else she had to say.

"Well, I was sitting there when the bell on the door jingled. I looked up and it was Ryan. He was with another woman, his arm was around her neck and he kissed her on the cheek." She could hear Tiffany's breathing on the other end, and wondered what she was thinking, if she was angry. "Tiffany?"

"I'm here. Why didn't you tell me this before now?"

"We weren't talking and I didn't want to make you even angrier at me by telling you this."

"I don't know. I'm confused right now."

"Well, um, maybe you guys had broken up already." Marisa was trying to smooth things over a bit.

"No, we hadn't. I mean, like, I understand and all. I wasn't there. That's a lot of distance between two people."

Marisa sat quietly not knowing what to say. She wondered if maybe she should have kept what she knew to herself.

"Anywhooo, I will see you in a few weeks, lady." Tiffany tried to move on from the conversation about Ryan. "I don't know exactly what date but I will try and call you. I gotta go now."

Her friend was hurting, Marisa could tell, and she felt badly for causing it. What she was doing now was just an excuse to get off the phone. "Okay. Can't wait to see you."

"Yeah, same here. Love you, bye."

"Bye, Tiff."

Marisa laid back on the bed. "Shoot, shoot, shoot!. Why didn't I just keep my big mouth shut?"

Feeling regret for telling Tiffany about what she saw, she lay motionless. Staring at the blades on the ceiling fan, Marisa focused on the quiet humming of the motor. With a sense of calm and sheer exhaustion, she was soon fast asleep.

Marisa was awakened by the sound of her ringing cell phone. With her eyes still closed, she felt around on the bed in an effort to smother the now escalating sound. Unable to determine where it was she opened her eyes.

Raising from the bed she looked around it before turning to look on the nightstand. Suddenly she realized the phone was still inside her purse from last night and reached inside just as it stop ringing.

"Oh well," Marisa said with a sense of complacency.

She laid back on the bed. Her face was partially buried in the purple and white duvet and her right hand hung down over the side of the bed. The phone rang again and this time Marisa quickly grabbed the phone to answer.

"Hello?"

"Hi there." The voice on the other end was unfamiliar.

Marisa pulled the phone back to look at the caller ID. There was no name. Just an unfamiliar number.

"Is this Marisa?"

"Um, yes. I..." she hesitated. "My apologizes, but are you sure you have the right Marisa?"

"I'm pretty sure, little lady."

Marisa froze at those words. Only one person called her "little lady" and for a brief second she felt dazed, as if she had been hit by a sledgehammer. Her breathing became panicked as she struggled with the idea that the man who had followed her to her dorm and raped her was on the other end of the phone.

"How did you get my number?"

"Your friend, Sam."

"Samantha? *She* gave you my number?"

"Why, yeah. I hope it was okay. I nearly twisted her arm to get it out of her."

Marisa stood up and began pacing back and forth. She knew she couldn't let on that she knew. She pulled the phone from her ear and took deep breathes, counting to ten.

"You there?"

Marisa placed the phone back to her ear just in time to hear Matt's question. "Um, yes, yes, I'm here. What do you want?"

"Well, I saw you last night and was wondering why you left so quickly. I didn't get the chance to say hello. Haven't had a chance to really talk to ya since graduation night."

Marisa felt almost suspended in time as her head started spinning. Matt's voice sounded like it was in slow motion.

"Why didn't you come to the party? I looked for ya..."

Marisa knew she had to keep up the charade. She didn't want Matt to detect anything. "I got a migraine all of a sudden," she let out a slight chuckle. "I guess it was the excitement of the night. I just couldn't shake it."

"Wow, that's cruel, lil lady. Course you didn't really miss anything. It had already started when I got there."

"Really? Um, what time did you go?"

She had thought to herself that maybe she could get as much information out of him as she could about that night.

"Oh, I don't really know. Probably around eleven o'clock, I think."

Again, Marisa tried to draw a timeline in her head but was too overwhelmed to put it all together so quickly. She wondered if it was him who followed them after the party last night. If it was, he now knew where she lived. As Matt continued talking, she could hear a faint beep. Pulling the phone from her ear, she saw another call coming in. It was Patrick. A sense of relief came over her. Here was her chance to get off the phone with Matt.

"I'm sorry, I have an important call coming through."

He stopped talking. "Oh, okay, lil lady. Well, I'll catch up with you soon, I hope—"

Marisa had clicked over before Matt could finish his sentence. "Hello, Patrick."

"Well, hello. I see you made it home okay."

"Yes, we did. I'm sorry I had to leave so abruptly."

"Nah, no worries. So was your friend okay?"

"My friend?" Marisa's head was still reeling from the conversation with Matt. "Oh, my friend, Sam. Yes, she's fine. She may have a bit of a hangover." She laughed sheepishly, the anxiety she was feeling finally began to taper off.

"So, I was wondering, maybe we can get together for dinner next weekend."

Marisa was taken by surprise when she heard Patrick's invitation. "Well, I don't have any plans. I'd be glad to."

"Great! So would you like for me to pick you up? We can go to the tavern where I saw you that night."

"Oh, that would be nice. I live at 4949 Cobblestone Street."

"Cool. I'll see you then."

"Okay, Patrick. See you Saturday."

Marisa hung up the phone. She sat on the bed for a moment. Her mind had already wandered into next weekend. "Boy, I need a cup of coffee."

Just as she was about to put on a pot of coffee, her phone rang again. Picking it up from the nightstand where she placed it, she saw that it was Patrick again. She hurried to answer it.

"Hello?"

"Hello there. I forgot to tell you what time."

"Oh, that's right. We didn't say what time, did we?"

"No, I didn't. So pick you up at six o'clock?"

"Okay, that sounds good."

"See you then."

Patrick had hung up as fast as he had called. She placed the phone on the bed and headed towards the kitchen. Her mind wandered back to the the party and seeing Matt talking with Samantha.

"Ouch!"

Marisa quickly pulled her hand back from under the faucet. She had accidentally turned on the hot water valve instead of the cold. She shook her hand in the air and then pulled it back to look at it. It was already turning red.

"Oh, this is just great. I can't even make a pot of coffee without giving myself a first degree burn." Marisa chuckled to herself. *Well, as long as it's okay by Saturday I guess I can live with it. Worse things could happen.*

Marisa continued her day, not realizing that what she had just spoken was actually a prediction.

The next morning Samantha showed up bright and early to pick her up for work. Still standing in the mirror putting on her makeup, Marisa heard the car horn outside. She looked at the clock on the bedroom wall. Picking up the pace, she finished her makeup, grabbed her purse and headed for the door. She was still trying to put on her shoes as she hopped towards the car.

"You're running kinda behind, I see."

Marisa gasped for her breathe. "Yeah, I tossed and turned last night. I just couldn't sleep."

"Well, after a night like Saturday, I could understand why."

"Yeah, you have no idea."

There was a brief silence as Samantha headed onto the on ramp. "Um, Marisa, I..." she stopped as Marisa looked towards her, waiting for her to continue.

"Yes, Sam? What is it?"

She took a deep breath before continuing. "Um, this morning on the news, there was a report..."

"Okay, what kind of report?" Marisa had now focused intently on her. "What report?"

"There was a rape in our area Saturday night."

A lump swelled in Marisa's throat. Unable to utter a word, she just sat there in shock.

"Marisa?" She looked over at her, a look of disbelief still masking her face. "Marisa?"

"Did...I mean, who? Did they catch the person? Tell me, Sam!" The conversation became intense.

"No. They said she was walking home alone. Apparently she had just left from the tavern restaurant."

Marisa was visibly shaking.

"I'm sorry. I should have waited until after work to tell you."

Marisa turned and sat back in her seat. "That's down the street from me."

"Right, that's why I thought you should know." As Samantha continued down the highway, she glanced over at Marisa again. "What are you thinking?"

"Why…?" She started to say, but hesitated.

"I don't know. It's crazy."

"No, Sam. I mean, why, why did you give Matt my number?"

A look of confusion came across Samantha's face. "What do you mean?"

"He called me. You should have never given him my number."

"I—I thought if you guys were friends, and you only suspected him…maybe there was a chance that you were mistaken if you talked it out."

"We went to the same college together but we hardly spoke that much."

"He just seems like a really nice guy."

"They always seem nice. But I mean, you never really know people. You never know what's in their hearts or their minds until one day they violate your trust."

Marisa dropped her head. Tears fell from her eyes and onto her burgundy skirt.

"Marisa, I'm so sorry. I shouldn't have given your number out like that, not to him."

For the rest of the ride no one said another word. Pulling into the parking lot Samantha parked in a spot near the front entrance of the building. They sat still for a few minutes, silence echoing loudly inside the car.

Samantha took a deep breath. "I'm sorry, Marisa."

Now a bit calmer, she looked over at Samantha. "I know. I should not have yelled. You weren't sure."

She reached over and grabbed Marisa's hand. "Friends?"

She managed a slight smile. "Sure thing."

"So, in light of what I told you, are you going to be okay? At work, I mean."

"Yeah, sure, Sam. I'll be fine." She grabbed the handle and opened the door.

"Oh, you want to have lunch today?"

Marisa thought for a second. "Um, no, not today. I have somewhere I need to go."

With a look of curiosity, Samantha relented. "Oh, okay, I will try to catch you at break, or something. If not, I will see you after work."

"Okay, thanks, Sam."

"No problem."

The girls exited the car and walked inside the building together. The day went by fairly quickly. After work, they both stopped by a well-known lounge called *After Six* for cocktails. After being seated, they both ordered drinks and resumed their earlier talk about the rape that had occurred in their quaint little town.

"So, do you think this incident had anything to do with that strange car that was parked on the street?"

Marisa shrugged her shoulders. "I don't know. It could just be coincidental." She didn't want to sound paranoid.

"Yeah, maybe you're right. I know it's unsettling. We've never had anything like this happen before." Samantha, hesitating to bring up the subject of Marisa's rape, felt like she had to ask her about that night. "Marisa, I have to ask..."

Looking at the waiter coming in their direction, she turned to give Samantha her full attention. "What?"

She was about to ask the question when the waiter approached their table.

"Martini?"

Samantha slightly raised her hand. The waiter placed the drink in front of her.

"And Marble and Lime for you, ma'am."

Marisa smiled at the waiter as he placed her drink on the table. Focusing back on Samantha, she encouraged her to continue.

"I hate to bring this up, again. I know it's a pretty painful thing to recall, but have you gotten any counseling? I mean, I'm not trying to pry. But sometimes these kinds of things have a way of affecting your life. Even when you don't think it is."

Marisa sipped on her drink then took a deep breath. "I'm okay. I don't need to speak to anyone."

Samantha pressed a bit more. "Um, other than me, I mean. I ask because it's important, Marisa. Did you report the incident to the police?"

She chuckled sarcastically. "Really, Samantha? College campus, big graduation night with a party at some Fraternity house? Who was I going to tell? Who was going to believe me? I wasn't going to be humiliated more by saying something."

"But it didn't happen at some Frat house, Marisa, it happened in your dorm."

"Yes, and the first thing someone will say is, I took someone back to the dorm or—or I shouldn't have been walking in the dark. No, thank you, Sam. That night was like a nightmare. I go to sleep at night and my dreams are tortured with memories. Sometimes I wake up in a cold sweat and the smell of his woodsy cologne seems to engulf the whole room when—"

"His cologne?" Samantha interjected. "You mean you remember the fragrance?"

"As if it were yesterday."

"You said woodsy. Like a deep or subtle woodsy?"

"More subtle, I guess. It wasn't overpowering. Just enough to..." Marisa paused for a second. "Why?" She was now looking at Sam with curiosity.

Samantha's face had a look of shock. "Well, Matt had on a subtle woodsy cologne the other night. I actually complimented him on it."

Marisa's eyes widened. With her drink already up to her mouth, she slowly placed the glass on the table as they both stared at each other in silence.

Marisa and Samantha sat quietly on their way home. The sound from the passing cars echoed like rushes of wind. Neither of them quite knew what to make of the information they had just shared. Marisa would periodically roll her thumbs around each other as she clasped her purse snugly in her lap.

"So what do you plan to do now, Marisa? I mean this is crazy and scary."

"I don't know. I don't know if there is anything that I *can* do."

"I mean, I know you're in London and it didn't happen here, but there has got to be something you can do. You can't live in fear the rest of your life."

"I don't plan to."

Samantha glanced over at her. "What do you mean?"

Marisa looked up. "I, I can't say, well, at least not right now."

Samantha was even more confused. Just as she was about to ask another question, Marisa's phone rang. Grabbing it, she placed one finger in the air signaling for her to pause the conversation for a moment. "Hello?"

"Hi, Rissa!"

"Oh my God, Tiff!" It had been several days since they had the opportunity to talk.

"How're things in the beautiful scenic place called London?"

"Things are good," she answered with some hesitancy.

"Okay, what's up, girl?"

"What do you mean?"

"Marisa, how many times do we have to do this drill?"

"Drill? What drill?"

"The how-long-I've-been-knowing-you drill and the bff drill…?"

"Oh, we're still best friends?" she smiled as she looked over at Samantha. "I mean, like, since you've been in the states and well, I haven't heard from you, I decided to get a new bff."

"Really? It's like that?"

"Mm-hmm," Marisa chuckled. "Well, just for that, I was about to tell you when I was flying in…"

"What?!" Marisa bounced lightly in her seat. "When—when will you be here?"

"Ohhh, no. I'm not telling you now. I might just stay here in the states."

"Come on, Tiffany. When?" she placed her hand slightly over the phone and her other hand on Samantha's elbow. "This is my best friend."

"I gathered," she said as she glanced over at her.

"Who are you talking to, Rissa?"

"I'm with—" Marisa stopped. "I'm not telling unless you tell me when you're coming in." She didn't hear a sound on the other end. She looked to see if she had lost the connection, then placed the phone back to her ear. "Hello? Hello?"

"Ha! Gotcha! And no I'm not telling you. I will say, though, it will be soon."

"Ughh. I know how stubborn you can be so I won't ask again. I'm just excited you'll finally be here." A look of perplexity came across Marisa's face. "Wait, you've got to tell me when you'll be here, otherwise you'll be stuck at the airport."

"Really, Rissa?" Tiffany sounded a bit baffled that she had even made the statement. "Um, I have a way to get from the airport."

"How? You can't seriously be thinking about catching a—" Marisa stopped.

"Wait! Do I hear the sound of the elevator going up?"

"Oh, shut up, Tiffany. I forgot…Ryan," The girls said in unisons. "By the way, how is Ryan?"

"He's good."

"So, like, are you two back on?"

"Well, I don't know. We will see once I'm there."

The car slowly pulled up to the sidewalk in front of Marisa's apartment. "Hold on, Tiffany."

"Sure thing."

Marisa turned towards Sam. "Thanks so much. See you tomorrow?"

She smiled and nodded her head. "Take care, love."

"Thanks, Sam." Marisa exited the car and waved as she drove off down the street. Once inside the house, she resumed her conversation. "So, have you seen or talked with my mom?"

"Actually, I haven't...have you?"

Marisa made her way to the bedroom. She sat on the edge of the bed as she removed her shoes. "No, I haven't talked with her. I haven't been calling."

"What? Why? Come on, Marisa, that's your mom."

She laid back on the bed. "I know. It's just that there is so much going on right now. I can't take on my mom and dad right now."

"What do you mean?"

"Well, most times I *do* talk to her, it's always something about dad not being there and always out of town. I don't have the heart to tell her what I saw."

"What you *saw*?"

"Yeah, remember when I told you about the Sorority trip?"

"Oh, yeah. I forgot about that."

"I'm sure he was banging her, as well."

"Rissa! You don't know that. It may not be what you thought you saw at all."

"Tiffany, my dad's living a double life. He comes home, tells mom he has to take these out of town trips and she believes him. I don't trust men, period... Well, enough about that. So, when did you say you were flying in?" There was a brief silence that made Marisa look at her phone again to see if she had lost the connection, then put it back to her ear. "Hello?"

"I'm here."

"Everything okay, Tiff?"

"Yeah, I was just thinking about your question?"

"My question?"

"Uh-huh, I don't think I ever told you when I was flying in."

The girls burst into laughter.

"Ooo, I can't stand you, Tiffany!"

"I know, I know. I love you too, girl. Well, I need to go. I have a lot of packing and things I need to do today."

"Right. You sure you don't want to tell me, you know, so I can be prepared?"

"Nope, no can do, girly. Gotta go."

"Okay. Can't wait for you to get here."

"Me too, Rissa. Well, ciao bella."

"Bye, Tiff."

Marisa laid her phone on the bed. Sitting up she knocked her purse on the floor. Hesitating, she looked at the purse as it lay on the floor. She slowly reached down to pick it up, then laid the purse on the bed and stared at it for a moment.

Her hand slid inside it and pulled out the gun that was concealed within it. It was the one she had seen at the gun store. She had gone there during her lunch break to purchase it.

Although she had taken the safety course, Marisa was still unsure about the purchase. After hearing of the rape, her fear and anxieties increased. Even more apparent was the rage she had begun to feel. She had promised herself that no one would ever take advantage of her like that again.

9
Delusions May Come

The week seemed to drag by. Marisa was excited, but nervous about meeting up with Patrick. Walking out of the office building, she sat on a nearby bench as she waited for Samantha.

Her thoughts wandered back to college and how exciting her junior year was. It was the first time she had seen Patrick on campus. She was at the campus's café studying for finals when he approached where she was sitting.

"Well, who do we have here?"

Marisa looked up from her books. Looking around, she pointed to herself. "Who me?"

"Yeah, you. Where have you been all my life?"

"Probably getting an education. You should, too."

"Ooohhh! Quick on the sarcasm, huh?"

Marisa kept studying.

"So, whatcha studying?"

She sighed. "I'm studying for my finals."

Patrick looked over at her book. "Oh, foreign languages. Yeah, I'm taking that one, too."

"Well, shouldn't you be somewhere studying it?"

"Hey, I don't have to study. I'm a football star. I'm Patrick Weston."

Marisa glared up at him. Sighing at his remark, she started putting her books inside her backpack. "Well, you must not be too popular. I've never heard of you." She then stood up, slinging her sack over her shoulder.

"Hey, where you going?"

Looking back over her shoulder, Marisa smiled as she kept walking.

"Oh, it's like that?"

She waved her hand in the air as she walked out the door...

Marisa was startled out of her daydream by Samantha's voice. "Marisa!"

"I'm sorry, Sam."

"Where were you? That must have been a pretty awesome place."

Marisa chuckled. "I was thinking about my junior year in college."

"Must have been pretty amazing."

She looked up at her. "It was."

"You ready?"

"Yeah. You know I was wondering if we could stop in the market place. I'd like to get something to wear Saturday night."

"Oh, that's right. You have a perky date with ummm…" Samantha struggled to remember his name.

"Patrick, his name's Patrick."

"Oh yeah, right. Patrick. He's a bit cocky, isn't he?"

Marisa smiled. "A bit? He's a *lot* cocky and has been that way since school."

"Like I said before, you seem a bit smitten over him." Samantha clicked the button on her keys to unlock the car.

"No, I'm not *smitten*, as you put it."

"Then what is it then? Why are you going out with him?"

She hesitated. "You know…I don't know. It all happened so fast. I just said yes. I mean, I was a bit intrigued with him in school; the popular guy thing; him trying to talk to me. I shut him down a few times."

Samantha laughed. "Bet he didn't like that too much."

"Why do you say that?"

"Usually guys like that don't like to be told no."

Marisa thought for a minute. "He's cocky and all, but he's never showed me that he was angry. He had a girlfriend, well, at least I saw him with one, or two, when we were in college."

She looked over at Samantha as they both laughed. Playfully, she pushed the other girl's arm. "I just wasn't interested in an athlete with all his female entourage."

"Yeah, never settle for a man with an entourage. They're slimy." They laughed again. "Oh, Marisa, I know this great department store in the Brick. I'm sure you'll find something there."

"Cool. Let's go."

The girls arrived at the market moments later. Samantha looked feverishly for a place to park. "This is my least favorite part about coming here."

Marisa looked around. "I love coming here. It's like a whole different world. The people, the food, the shops. It's like being somewhere far away from home."

"Um, news flash, Marisa, you *are* far away from home."

She looked over at Samantha then burst out laughing. "Oh yeah, I am. Look, a parking space!" A car pulled away just in time for Samantha to pull right in.

"Alright!" she gave Marisa a high-five. "Good looking out, Ms. Thing. Oh, and there's the store I wanted to take you to right there."

Marisa looked in the direction she was pointing. "Mia's Boutique. Cute name. I hope cute clothes."

They got out of the car and headed towards the boutique. Marisa took a deep breath. "Smell that awesome food."

"Yeah, the food here is quite good. Maybe we can get some when we're done."

"Oh, that sounds wonderful."

They made their way inside the boutique. Vintage blouses lined one wall. Various formal gowns lined another. The floor held racks of modern and vintage wear, and a place for shoes was nestled to the back of the store. The array of styles and colors grabbed Marisa's attention. She picked up a pair of blue pumps.

"Ooooh, these are nice." She turned towards Samantha, but the girl was too busy looking at dresses. Shrugging her shoulders, she turned back only to notice a familiar face. The woman looked up from the vintage blouses she was perusing, giving Marisa a better view of her face.

"Indra?" Marisa said cautiously.

The young woman took a second glance in Marisa's direction, a smile spreading across her face. "Yes?"

"I think I met you at the club. You're Ryan's sister, right?"

"Yes, oh, I remember. I apologize though. I'm good with faces, not so much with names."

"Well, I'm Marisa. My best friend, Tiffany, was dating Ryan when we met."

"That's right! I do remember you now. How are you?"

"I'm good. How's Ryan?"

"He's fine. We're planning a family trip to Hawaii. I've been shopping for the trip."

"Wow! That sounds amazing. So when are you going?"

"In about three weeks. I don't like last-minute packing so that's why I'm here."

"Tiffany is supposed to be back soon."

"Yes, I heard. Ryan told me."

"Oh, he did?" Marisa thought this was her opportunity to find out exactly when Tiffany would be arriving. "So, did she tell him what day she'd be flying in?"

"Actually, he didn't mention the exact day. Just that she'd be flying in soon. She didn't tell you?"

"Well, no she didn't."

"Then she wants to surprise you," she said, smiling suddenly. "And here you are being sneaky and trying to get the information from me."

They laughed together.

"Yeah, I guess I was."

"I actually peeled off from Ryan and Mum about an hour ago. Oh! We took a picture." Indra pulled her cell phone from her purse. Scrolling through images she found the picture to show Marisa. "Here we are. That's my mum." She pointed to the lady in the picture.

Marisa gasped. It was the woman she had seen Ryan with at the coffee shop. "That's your mother?"

"Yeah, isn't she beautiful? Sometimes, when people first meet her, they don't believe she'll be sixty-one soon."

"Sixty what? You're kidding, right?" Marisa looked at the picture again. "I saw them at the coffee shop down from where I worked a few weeks ago."

"On Bank Street? Yeah, my mum love's the coffee there." Indra stared at the picture. "I remember being around eleven or so...she would always ask me to make coffee for her."

Marisa smiled. "She is beautiful."

"Yes, she is...and strong. My mum had cancer, you know."

Caught off guard by what Indra said, she struggled to find the right words to say. "Indra, I'm—I'm so sorry."

"Thank you. She's actually in remission. What I love about her, though, is her strength. You would never know because she's such a gracious and loving person. She's always smiling."

They continued to look at the picture when Samantha walked up.

"Hi. You find anything?"

"No. Not yet, Sam. Oh, forgive my manners. Tiffany's boyfriend has a sister who lives here, too. This is Indra."

"Hi, pleased to meet you." Indra reached out to take Samantha's extended hand. "Well, I'd better get going." She began walking towards the cash register as she looked down at her watch. "I'm supposed to meet back up with Ryan and Mum in about ten minutes." Looking over at Samantha. "It was a pleasure meeting you."

"Same here."

They both smiled and waved goodbye as Indra walked out the door.

"Tell Ryan I said hello."

"Will do, Marisa. Bye."

Marisa looked at Samantha with a look of embarrassment. "Okay, what's wrong with you?"

She shook her head slowly. "Sam, I saw Ryan a few weeks ago at that little coffee shop we go to on Bank Street. When he came in he was with this woman... He had his arm around her neck..."

"Okay. Well, did he see you?"

"No, he didn't see me. I made sure of that, but, well, the next time I saw him, I was really mean. I mean, I went off. I even threatened the poor guy."

Samantha continued to listen, but Marisa could see the look of confusion on her face. "I thought he was cheating on my best friend."

"Okay then. So why the doom and gloom look?"

"Sam...he wasn't cheating. It was his mother!"

Samantha gasped as she put her hand over her mouth and chuckled.

Marisa glared at her. "It's not funny!" she said, slightly pushing the girl in the shoulder.

Slowly removing her hand from her mouth, she tried to stop laughing. "I'm sorry. So it was his Mum, eh?"

"Yes! And I told Tiffany that the poor guy was cheating on her."

Now, Samantha burst into laughter, and this time she laughed herself to tears.

"You're so mean, Sam!"

"I'm sorry, I can't help it. It's funny as bloody hell!"

Marisa couldn't help herself and was soon laughing along with her. "I can't stand you."

The girls continued laughing as they walked up to the register to pay for their items. Soon they were out the door.

That night Marisa tossed and turned in her sleep. She saw herself running as she was being chased by a dark shadow. It was the same dream she had been having since that horrible night. At times the figure was close enough to touch her as she found herself trying to run even faster.

But the dark figure that had seemed to outpace her in prior dreams was now standing with her, face to face. The distorted figure slowly reached out and placed it's dark cold hands over her mouth. Gasping for air, Marisa awakened from her sleep with a scream.

Sweat drenched the long shirt she was wearing to sleep in. She laid there for a while staring up in the ceiling, her heart racing inside her chest. The room looked ominous.

The shadow of the swaying tree just outside her bedroom window reflected on the wall at the other end of her room. She could hear the sound of the ice-maker as the ice fell into the bucket. She looked toward the bedroom door that she often left open.

The shadows played hallucinatory games with her eyes, because she was certain she saw something moving near the fireplace. Jumping up, she quickly went to the door. She gently closed it as if not wanting to alert whatever was in the living room.

Locking the door, she sneaked back and hopped into bed. Laying back she pulled the covers up to her chin with both her hands. She noticed a light on the ceiling that seemed to fade in and out.

Following the light, her eyes landed on her cell phone that was charging on the night stand. She grabbed the phone and dialed a familiar number. The phone rang. Anxious, Marisa waited for the person to pick up on the other end, but there was no answer.

"Tiffany where are you?" She dialed another number. "Hello? Hi...Mom?"

"Hi, Marisa, honey. How are you?"

"I'm great, Mom. I, um, was just calling to see how you were doing."

"Oh, I'm doing okay, honey."

"Good, good. How's Dad?" Marisa continued to make small talk to get her through the night.

"Well, um..."

Marisa could hear the hesitation in her mother's voice. "What's wrong? Is Daddy okay?"

"Yes, yes, he's okay. Honey, I have something to tell you."

Her heart felt as if it was in her throat as she anticipated her mother's next words. "Tell me what, Mom?"

"Honey, I didn't want to say anything, well, at least not yet."

"Mom, what is it?"

"Well..."

Marisa took a deep breath.

"Your father and I are getting a divorce."

Her mother's voice seemed to echo across the phone.

"A divorce?" Marisa thought for a moment, but found no empathy for her father. Keeping her father's secrets to herself she wondered how it had come to this point. "So, Mom, did Daddy ask for the divorce?" She could hear her mother take a deep breath on the other end.

"No, honey. I filed."

"You filed?" Marisa could not believe what her ears were hearing.

"Yes, I couldn't live the lie any longer, Marisa. I knew your father was cheating. I just didn't know how to handle it without hurting you. I finally came to this solution now that you're gone. I want to be happy. I'm so sorry, Rissa, baby."

Oddly, she felt a sense of relief. She loved her father and had always thought her mother was choosing to be blind. For the first time she realized her mother was one of the strongest women she had ever known; sacrificing her own happiness to protect her daughter's.

"So, where is Daddy now? I mean, is he still at the house?"

"No. He moved out over a month ago. He went to California."

Marisa's mind wandered back to the night she saw her father. "Mom, I saw Daddy there, in California. It was the night I went for the Sorority convention. I..." she hesitated. "I saw him with someone. He didn't see me. And I never said anything, because I just didn't know how to tell you."

"That's okay. I knew."

Marisa was surprised. "You knew?"

"Yes, I knew. I actually met her at one of your father's business trips. He, of course, didn't know I knew until I told him."

"Wow, Mom. I'm so sorry."

"No, it's not your fault. Sometimes people just grow apart. We just...grew apart. We are amicable now and knew this was the right thing for the both of us."

Marisa smiled. It meant the world to discover that her mother wasn't weak as she had always thought but, in fact, stronger than she thought she could ever be.

"Mom, have I told you lately that I love you?" She could hear her mother laughing through her tears. "I knew about Dad. It's just that all this time, I thought you felt you didn't deserve better. I was so angry at you because, well, I thought you were signing off on his infidelities by being docile. I'm so proud of you, Mom, for finally getting to a place of living your life and, hopefully, finding someone who will love and respect you for the beautiful person you are."

"Marisa, you're the best daughter a mother could ever hope for."

"Aww, thanks, Mom. So, when are you coming to London?"

"As soon as all the loose ends are tied up here. I hope really soon."

"That would be great, Mom." A thought then came across her mind. "Have you talked with Tiffany lately?"

Her mother thought for a moment. "You know, I did, just the other day. She said she was getting ready to come back to London."

"Oh? Did she happen to say when she was flying back?" Marisa was trying to pin down the answer that Tiffany or Indra would not give her earlier.

"Well, honey, Tiffany said you'd probably ask if I spoke with you. She asked me not to say."

"Ahhh, come on, Mom!"

"Nope, no can do," she laughed.

"You guys are the worst."

"I know, honey, I know. Talk soon. Bye," her mother laughed again before hanging up.

By now daybreak was making it's still dimly lit appearance from underneath Marisa's bedroom door. The warmth of the rising London sun could be felt through the window. She laid back on the bed and for a moment she had forgotten all about the dream. She smiled. This was the first time that she could ever remember her mother being truly happy.

The morning seemed to have come as quickly as the prior evening had gone. Exhausted from the nightmares, Marisa couldn't help but wonder why they were getting worst. Sitting up on the side of the bed, she stretched for a moment, then stood to her feet.

Walking towards the bathroom, she caught a glimpse of the purse where she had placed the gun. Remembering how she always felt about owning one, she shivered at the thought of ever having to use it.

Images invaded her thoughts. The room seemed to fade in the distance as they intensified. Suddenly a sharp buzzing sound echoed from the kitchen. Startled, Marisa realized she was still standing in the middle of the room. She took a deep breath and continued towards the bathroom.

Soon the aroma of freshly brewing hazelnut coffee was making its way through the apartment. The smell seemed to invigorate her as she walked out of the bathroom and into the kitchen. "Nothing like a spot of coffee." She said aloud, giggling at the sound of her saying *spot*.

Well, today is the day, Patrick Weston. I can't believe I even accepted the invitation to go out with his arrogant...

Marisa heard the faint sound of her cell phone ringing in the bedroom. Walking quickly, she reached the phone before it stopped ringing. "Hello...hello?" She could tell someone was on the other end but there was no response. She hung up as she stood there gazing at the phone.

"Humph! Wrong number, I guess."

Marisa headed back towards the kitchen with her phone in hand. As she picked up her coffee cup, the phone rang again. For a moment she pondered if she should answer. She took a sip from her cup as she looked at the flashing light from the incoming call. Placing her cup on the counter she grabbed the phone.

"Hello?"

"Hello there."

"Patrick?" Marisa was visibly caught off guard. He was the last person she expected to be on the other end.

"Good morning." His voice sounded husky and deeper than what she remembered. "I was, um, just lying here, thinking."

"Really? About what, Mr. Weston?"

Patrick chuckled. "...About seeing you tonight."

"I'm looking forward to it as well." Marisa tried not to come across as nervous.

"So, what are you wearing?"

"Excuse me?" His question caught her off guard.

"What are you wearing? Tonight?"

"Oh, tonight." Marisa chuckled nervously.

"Yeah. What did you think I was talking about?"

"Oh. Nothing. I guess I'm still trying to wake up. You know, got to get that cup of coffee." Marisa was too embarrassed to say what she was really thinking.

"So, your girl is still in the states, huh?"

"Who? Tiffany?"

"Yeah, that's her name. You guys were always together on campus."

"Yep, that's my girl. She's still in the states. She said she's flying in soon but she wouldn't tell me when."

"Oh, really? So you've been home alone, huh?"

"Kinda. My co-worker, Samantha, and I have been hanging pretty tight since I've been here."

"Samantha..." Patrick thought for a second. "Oh, that's the inebriated one from the party," he chuckled.

"Stop it, Patrick. She was just having a good time."

"I'm just kidding. Good thing she had you there as a friend, seeing as how you don't live that far from each other."

"What do you mean?"

"She lives in the same area as you, right? I mean, I assumed since you said you were driving her home."

"Oh, right. I did." Thoughts of that night began to run through Marisa's mind. She couldn't help but think about the car that had parked down the street as she wondered.

"Patrick." Marisa hesitated. Her heart raced inside her chest as she thought of the question she was about to ask. "What kind of car do you drive?"

"What kind of car? Why?"

Marisa didn't want to tell him exactly why she had asked. "I mean, you *are* picking me up tonight, right?" To her surprise, he started laughing.

"You're wondering if I'm going to be picking you up in a hoop-dee, huh?" he continued laughing.

"No, no. I'm not superficial like that."

"Well, you must have changed from college, girl."

"What do you mean?"

Patrick laughed through his sentence. "You always acted as if you were too good to hang out with the rest of us."

Marisa was taken aback by what he said. "I never thought that, Patrick." For a moment the conversation seemed to have taken a different direction. Marisa felt uncomfortable.

"Okay, I'm sorry. Come on. I was just joking. Lighten up."

Marisa tried to play off her feelings by brushing him off.

"By the way, I have a black Beemer. I'll be picking you up in style."

"Oh, wow! Now I don't have to worry about lying back in the seat so no one sees me," she chuckled, hoping to break the awkwardness that had entered the conversation moments ago.

"Well, I wouldn't be driving around in anything that doesn't reflect my swag."

Marisa shook her head. "One thing I can definitely say hasn't changed about you."

"What's that?" Patrick said, curious to hear her response.

"You're still arrogant."

He laughed out loud. "I'm not arrogant."

She already knew what his response was going to be.

"Yeah, I know. I'm just confident."

They both said at the same time. Marisa rolled her eyes playfully as she smiled. Suddenly she pulled the phone back from her ear to check the time.

"Whoa!"

"What? What's wrong?" Patrick asked with concern.

"The time."

"Yeah, what about it?"

"Well, Mr. Weston, if I'm going to be on time for tonight, I need to get off the phone."

There was a brief pause. "Oh dang. I lost track of the time. Yeah, gotta go, too, lil lady."

A piercing feeling came over Marisa. "Why did you say that?"

"Huh? Say what?" he said.

"I've never heard you use that phrase before."

"What phrase?"

Marisa felt a sinking feeling in the pit of her stomach. There had been only one other person who had called her that. "Why did you say *lil lady*?"

Patrick didn't answer right away. "I don't know. It's just what came out at the time. Why do you ask?"

Marisa thought maybe she was overreacting. "I just asked. I just thought you'd turned into a cowboy for a minute there." she laughed and tried to play it off as a joke.

"Well, ya just never know there, lil lady. I might have to rope ya a lil later and tie ya up," he said, sounding like a western cowboy.

Although Marisa felt uncomfortable, she went along. "Well, Patrick, I guess I will see you soon."

Through his laughter he said, "Yeah, seven sharp."

Marisa only chuckled lightly. "Seven sharp. Bye."

She sat still for a moment. Her nerves were unsettled as she thought about the phrase Patrick had just used. But she needed to pull herself together. Trying to push it out of her mind, she picked up her coffee cup and took another sip as she stared out the kitchen window.

"Ugh! Cold coffee, cold coffee," she yelped, and poured the coffee into the sink. She headed towards the bedroom to prepare for what she *hoped* would be a great evening.

Knowing Patrick would be picking her up in the next two hours, Marisa anxiously paced her bedroom. She walked over to her closet and for a moment she just stood there staring at the white silk blouse she had bought earlier that week. Laying it on the bed, she stepped back putting her right hand on her hip.

"This is too plain. Maybe I should wear something else."

She walked back to the closet. "Let's see. Maybe this dress. No, maybe this black one. Hell, I'm not going to a funeral." She turned back towards the bed where she had laid the blouse. "Okay, tag you're it, I guess."

Taking a deep breath, she slowly sat on the side of the bed.

Geez Tiff, I wish you were here. I feel so conflicted about going out on dates. At least you would be my voice of reason.

Marisa glared at the clock on the nightstand again. She grabbed the blouse and walked back to the closet. Pushing the clothes aside she came across a pair of mulberry-colored silk pants she had forgotten she had.

"Well, where have you been hiding?" she said as she removed the pants from the hanger, then laid them next to the blouse. "Okay, I can wear the pearls I got for—"

Marisa stopped. The pearls were a graduation gift from her father. She walked over to the jewelry box. Slowly opening the top, a soft musical ballad escaped the inside of it, and filled the room. Picking up the pearls she closed her eyes as she held them.

She brought the necklace close to her chest as she thought of her father. She remembered the times when her dad would pick her up in his arms and call her his little jewel. For a moment she forgot about the anxiousness she was feeling.

Daddy, I love you. I miss you so much. Marisa thought to herself. She opened her eyes as she placed the pearls on top of the dresser.

She then walked into the bathroom and grabbed a small makeup bag from the drawer of her vanity. Just as she began applying her makeup, she heard the sound of her cell ringing from inside her purse. She pulled the phone out of the outside pocket.

"Hello?"

"Hey there." It was Patrick. "I'm running a bit late. You mind meeting me there?"

Marisa hesitated for a moment. "Um, sure, sure. I'll see you in an hour, I guess."

"Cool. Hey, look, I apologize. I just got caught up in something and couldn't get away."

"Oh, that's okay."

"Okay, see you in a few." Patrick hung up.

A bit baffled, Marisa stood there for a moment staring at the now blank screen of her phone. Shrugging her shoulders, she laid it on top of the silk pants that were neatly laid out on the bed, and headed back to finish her makeup.

Now completely dressed, she looked at herself in the full length mirror that was nestled in the corner behind the bedroom door. She put her hands up around the top of the blouse to straighten the collar.

"Oh, my pearls!" She couldn't forget those!

She hurried over to the dresser and grabbed the necklace. Snapping them around her neck, she smiled as she turned to get a better view of how they looked on her. The mulberry-colored silk pants and white silk blouse shimmered as she turned from one side to the other.

"Okay. This is as good as it gets, girl."

Marisa grabbed a dark purple clutch from a small box in the closet. Just as she was about to walk out the door she ran back into the bedroom and grabbed her keys. "Guess you want to sleep outside tonight," Marisa said to herself. She closed and locked the door behind her.

The sun was just beginning to set as small flickers of starlight could be seen through the rays of a golden-orange hue. The gentle wind occasionally enveloped her hair, raising it from her shoulders. She brushed the wind blown strands from her face as she walked down the cobblestone street adjacent the sidewalk. This was her chance to reflect on the phone call from Patrick earlier.

Dang, I've heard of going dutch but this is dutch on steroids. Wonder what came up? Guess it was important.

Marisa continued her way down the sidewalk. Midway there, several old english cast-iron street lamps flickered as they lit up one by one. Soon she was standing at the door of the restaurant. Several cars were parked out on both sides of the now lighted streets. She saw people filing inside as soft music drifted outside. She pulled a small mirror from her purse to check her makeup.

"Well, here goes nothing," she murmured.

"Good evening, Mademoiselle. Reservation?"

Marisa wasn't sure how to answer the waiter's question. She had not discussed with Patrick if reservations needed to be made.

"Yes, Weston. Reservation for two." A voice came from just over her right shoulder.

"Very good, sir." The waiter scanned the book for Patrick's name.

Marisa turned to see him towering above her. With neatly groomed hair, his physique appeared even broader under the dark blue jacket and cream-colored cotton shirt. His denim jeans revealed thick thighs and chiseled calves. Though Marisa had seen him a few times since being in London, he looked much taller now than what she remembered.

"Dressed for success, I see," Marisa said playfully.

"Always," Patrick said looking down at her.

Soon the waiter walked up to them both. "This way, please."

They followed closely as the waiter seated them near the side of the stage. Patrick pulled out the chair for Marisa to be seated.

"Excuse me," he said to the waiter before he could walk away. "Will the band be playing tonight?"

The waiter nodded his head. "Yes, in fact, they are due to perform in fifteen minutes, sir."

"Thank you," Patrick said, allowing the waiter to continue back to the hostess counter. He unbuttoned his jacket as he seated himself at the table. "So, Marisa Webb. Finally."

Marisa smiled, nervously. "Finally." She looked around the restaurant. "You know, this is much nicer than what I remember."

Patrick looked around as well. "Hmm, I guess there is a different crowd here tonight. I mean, that night I saw you it was pretty late."

She thought for a minute. "Yeah, I think it was. The crowd seemed more rambunctious, for sure, like the couple you were with."

"The couple?" He looked confused.

"Yes, the couple you said you were with the night I saw you. They were having an argument or something…"

He snapped his fingers. "Oh yeah, yeah. That was a crazy night."

Marisa chuckled. "I could only imagine. So, did they ever make up?"

"Um, nah, don't think they did. Well, so what's been going on with you?" Patrick smoothly changed the subject. "I want to hear about the adventures of Marisa after college."

Smiling, she heard a noise behind her. Turning, she saw the band as they were taking the stage. "Oh, wow. The band's here."

"Yeah, maybe we can dance later."

"Yeah, sure."

Patrick sat there looking at her. "Sooo, how's things been since being here in London?"

"It's been okay. I've been working. I'm actually up for a promotion."

"Oh? What type of promotion?"

"Well, I've been offered a Junior Executive position in marketing."

Patrick smiled as he leaned forward. "That's amazing, little lady." A visible cord of apprehension ran throughout Marisa's body. He could see a change in her countenance. "Are you okay?"

Marisa was frozen where she sat as thoughts raced through her mind. She had never heard Patrick use that term so loosely with her before.

"Hello?"

Waving his hand in front of her face, his features slowly came back into focus.

"Oh, I'm sorry. I went into deep thought for a moment there."

"Well, that was pretty darn deep. What were you thinking about?"

"Nothing in particular." Marisa knew she couldn't tell him what she was really thinking.

After giving their order to the waitress, the band began playing *Forever Together.* Patrick said smilingly, "Would you like to dance, Ms. Webb?"

With thoughts still swirling in her mind, Marisa nodded yes. Patrick held out his hand for hers. Slowly she pushed the chair back as she raised from her seat. Several couples had already begun dancing out on the floor. Patrick hummed a few bars of the song as they danced. Pulling back he looked at Marisa.

"You know, when we were in college, I saw you quite often. I really thought you couldn't stand me. You always gave me this look."

She looked up at him. "What look?"

"Girl, a look like you could run over me with your car."

Marisa chuckled. "No, I just didn't want to be a part of the groupies that were always hanging around the football star."

"Well, what would have been wrong with that?"

She was surprised at his response. Shaking her head she looked off to the side. "I wasn't the groupie type."

Patrick laughed as he pulled her closer. "Not the groupie type, huh?"

Marisa became quiet at his gesture. Suddenly the scent of his cologne made her pull back.

"What's wrong?"

She felt paralyzed as she walked back to the table. "I wasn't ready for this." She grabbed her purse and started towards the door.

"Ready for what? Ready for what? What are you talking about?" Patrick stood there, helpless, as he watched Marisa walk out the door.

Thoughts swirled cyclone-like inside her mind as she headed down the sidewalk. She thought back to their conversation. The fact that he called her *"lil lady"* rushed back to her memory. Now the scent of his woodsy cologne was more than she could handle. Feelings of anxiety overwhelmed her as she made her way to the cobblestone street. Her heart raced inside her chest as she looked back towards the tavern.

"I should not have gone. I should not have gone," Marisa mumbled over and over.

All of a sudden she stumbled on a small pebble that had lodged itself in between the cobblestone street. She felt a sharp pain shoot through the back of her ankle. Grabbing her heel, she vigorously rubbed her ankle as if she was trying to rub the pain away.

With her ankle now throbbing, she limped up the slight hill towards her apartment. The rounded hobbit-like door, where a potted spider plant hung from a nail driven in the concrete, seemed much farther away than before. The purple vintage hanging pot and the array of daffodils and chrysanthemums somehow didn't bring that feeling of a welcoming and untainted home as she hopped from one step to the other.

Marisa braced herself against the wall by the door entrance when an eerie feeling came over her. She looked behind her but only saw a couple walking in the distance. Still feeling the sting in her ankle, she searched frantically inside her clutch purse for her keys. Unable to find them she looked, again, down the dimly lit road.

Mentally exhausted from over-thinking everything, Marisa slowly slid down the burgundy hobbit-like door of her apartment. With a lump swelling in her throat, she burst into tears, and buried her head in the palms of her hands. Mascara filled tears rolled down her cheeks, staining the silk white blouse she had pulled from her closet only hours ago.

She heard the sound again, and went very still, listening for any kind of noise. She quickly wiped her eyes to get a better look as she dug inside her purse once more for the keys. Lodged in a small tear of the purse lining she could feel the heart shaped key ring.

Still feeling the pain in her ankle, she slowly raised herself from the steps. Glancing once more into the dark, she unlocked the door and quickly closed it behind her.

The conversation of the evening was still playing in the back of her mind. Emotionally exhausted, Marisa slid to the floor, feeling safer now that she was inside. Rubbing her ankle, tears again began streaming down her cheeks when suddenly she heard the slow turning of the doorknob. She looked with fear as she stood gazing at the handle.

"Who's there?" Marisa said, slowly backing away from the door. "Who's there?" There was no answer from the outside.

Her mind started working quickly, and she made her way to the bedroom. The purse that held the gun was still draped around the post of the bed. She pulled it out and walked back to the bedroom door.

She focused on the doorknob. For a moment there was no sound then the knob began to rattle again. Marisa hit the light switch from where she stood as the door slowly opened. Only the light from the lamp pole pierced the darkness inside her apartment.

Marisa trembled in fear as she pointed the gun towards the door. Hearing a male voice as it swung open, she screamed as she pulled the trigger. The sound of gunfire shattered the quiet, and she witnessed a body falling to the floor, then heard a scream from the outside. Still shaking, Marisa cut on the light switch.

"Oh my God!" Tiffany stood over Ryan as he lay bleeding on the floor. "Marisa! What have you done?! Call 9-1-1! Hurry!"

The gun was now dangling at Marisa's side, she couldn't form a coherent thought. She was in shock.

"Indra, call an ambulance...now!" Tiffany said as she kneeled by Ryan's side.

Epilogue

Three months later, Marisa and Tiffany sat at a table at the Button Down Disco. They spoke of the last year and all that had happened. Neither of them thought that their lives would turn out the way that they had.

"So, how's therapy going, Rissa?"

Marisa, sipping on a glass of virgin mimosa, smiled and lowered the glass from her lips. "It's going well, actually. Dr. Michaels is amazing."

"That's great. I'm so proud of you."

"Yeah." Marisa looked off into the crowded dance floor, then back at Tiffany. "You know, it was hard going back to the states and filing that rape report. I was so torn and confused. I just felt so ashamed. I thought people wouldn't believe me or say it was my fault."

Marisa paused as she took a deep breath. "I realize now that I don't have to be ashamed about what happened to me and I had to stop blaming myself. The fear I felt was crazy. Anything that remotely seemed or felt like that night just made my life so miserable, I was so *paranoid*. And trying to suppress my thoughts and emotions only made things worst. I felt like I was fighting for my sanity," Marisa said, still looking over at her friend.

Tiffany shook her head in agreement. "I was really worried about you. At times I felt so helpless. I didn't know how to help you. That's why I'm glad you decided to get help." She reached across the table and clutched Marisa's hands.

"You know, Tiff, I've met a lot of incredible women in my sessions. To have this support group has been the best thing for me..." she hesitated. "I don't know if I could have survived this whole ordeal without you, too...and I can't stress enough how sorry I am about Ryan."

Tiffany's eyes became misty as she fought back tears. "It's been a hard journey for all of us, but we made it. You know, Marisa, sometimes ugly things happen to really good people." She giggled then. "My mom used to say: 'Life can be an amazing journey with plenty of hiccups. You just can't allow those hiccups to stop you from living.'"

"Spoken like the wise woman that she is," Marisa said as she gently tightened her hand into Tiffany's. "Thanks for being the most amazing friend."

"Well, of course I am." She smiled, then looked towards the dance floor. "Here comes the gang," Tiffany said as she smiled and waved her hand in the air.

Marisa turned to see Indra, Samantha, Patrick and Matt coming towards the table.

"What's up? What's up, ladies?" Indra reached out to embrace Marisa then Tiffany.

"Doing great," Marisa said gleefully. "Whats up, Matt? Looks like you and Sam are getting closer by the day." She winked at Samantha.

"Yeah, he's a pretty great guy." Samantha and Matt kissed each other on the cheek.

"Hi, Indra. No date tonight?" Tiffany said looking back towards the door.

"Oh, contraire mon ami," she replied back just as a six-foot two, handsome, brunette walked up and handed her a drink. "Everyone…this is Bryce."

Everyone welcomed him to the group.

The club had begun to fill up with party-goers, and exotic music filled the air as they all sat around talking.

"What, you guys starting this party without me?"

A voice came from behind Indra, and she turned around.

"But of course not, big brother. There is no party without you."

Ryan inched his way over to Tiffany. "Well, hi there. So um…" he started, then looked around. "What's a cutie like you doing sitting over here all alone?"

Tiffany smiled. "Well, if you get over here and sit beside me, I won't be."

Ryan smiled as he gave her a kiss.

"Omg! Get a room, will ya!" Indra said, shoving her brother in the shoulder.

Marisa looked over at Patrick. With a smile she patted the seat next to her. And with a smile, he sat down beside her.

After ordering drinks, they all moved in closer.

"Well, hear! Hear! The gang is all here!" Tiffany said, grinning and looking around the table.

Marisa smiled as she lifted her glass. "A toast!" she said, also looking around the table. "To friendship, survival-ship and love-ship. Because this ship might be sailing tonight," she said looking at Patrick.

Everyone laughed as they lifted their glasses.

"To friendships, survival-ships and sailing-ships," Tiffany said as she winked at Marisa.

"Hear! Hear!" everyone around the table said as they raised their glasses in the air.

About the Author

Goldia Felder delivers literature that brings both intrigue and suspense as well as awareness to social views of importance.

As a trained martial artist, she has worked with inner city youth, teaching them the importance of self-discipline. With a degree in Business Administration and Management, Goldia has also worked in the mental health field and continues to volunteer with domestic violence centers, raising awareness to the damaging effects of domestic abuse.

www.ingramcontent.com/pod-product-compliance
Lightning Source LLC
LaVergne TN
LVHW011153080426
835508LV00007B/378